Quiet Moments

for Caregivers

Quiet
Moments *for*
Caregivers

Betty Free

Tyndale House Publishers Inc., Wheaton, Illinois

Visit Tyndale's exciting Web site at www.tyndale.com

Focus on the Family is a registered trademark of Focus on the Family, Colorado Springs, Colorado.

Edited by Karin Stock Buursma

Cover designed by Jacqueline L. Noe

Interior designed by Melinda Schumacher

Library of Congress Cataloging-in-Publication Data

Free, Betty.
  Quiet moments for caregivers and their families / Betty Free.
    p. cm.
  Includes index.
  ISBN 0-8423-5377-1 (pbk.)
    1. Caregivers—Prayer-books and devotions—English.   2. Family—Religious life.
I. Title.
  BV4910.9 .F74 2002
  242'.4—dc21   2001003996

Printed in the United States of America

08   07   06   05   04   03   02
7   6   5   4   3   2   1

EINAR AND HELEN FREE
ON THEIR 60TH WEDDING ANNIVERSARY

To Dad—my hero: Dad, you were as wonderful as any earthly father could be. You understood me and cared about me. You taught me about God's love and, through your example, showed me how to accept and return that love. I know you spent many hours with Jesus during your lifetime, and now you have gone to be with him forever. I think you must be singing, playing your violin, and planting beautiful flowers—or doing the heavenly equivalent of those activities. You know I always loved you very much, yet I feel at peace now when I go to visit your grave. I love the words God gave me for your tombstone: *Not here—home with Jesus!* How thankful I am, Dad, to know that you are safe at home. Someday we'll be living together again, this time under our heavenly roof. Love, Betty

To Mom—my mentor: Mom, even though you're often not yourself anymore, I'll always remember the real you. I learned from you that true love is not dependent upon actions. Even when I disappointed you, I never had to wonder if you still loved me. Thank you for your unconditional love, a mirror of God's love for everyone. Mom, you always made me feel good about myself. And you showed me how important it is never to hurt anyone's feelings. You demonstrated that *JOY* comes from putting *J*esus first, *O*thers second, *Y*ourself last. You once said, "I know it's hard for you to take care of me sometimes." You told me, "I cry at night for you." Oh, my little Mama, I cry for you, too. But then I recall your prayers, and I know that God holds us close. Thank you, Mom, for all you've taught me. Love, Betty

TABLE OF

C O N T E N T S

Praying in Valleys and on Peaks: Prayers for Caregivers

	Note to the Reader	xiii
PRAYERS OF ADORATION	The one in charge	2
	All I need to know	3
	"And he had compassion on them"	4
	Now and forever	6
PRAYERS ABOUT LOVE AND FAMILY	The gift of family	8
	Total acceptance	10
	Prayer of St. Francis of Assisi	11
	Multiple relationships	12
	Serving each other	14
	Still learning	15
	An independent widow	16
PRAYERS ABOUT CHANGE	From kitchen to sofa	18
	God's perfect timing	19
	I'll take care of that, Dad	20
	Still my sweet mama?	22
	Home or nursing home?	24
	Different decisions	26
	The one constant in my life	28
PRAYERS ABOUT WORRIES AND FEARS	Facing my own changes	30
	No more worries	32
	Carefree days	34
	No reason	36
	It's your money, God	38

Prayers about
Pain and Suffering | I can't fix it anymore | 40
Making sense of it all | 42
Jesus by your side | 44
Doesn't God love me anymore? | 46
In the valley | 48
Fourteen years of care | 50

Prayers for
Forgiveness | It's not fair, God! | 52
Times are different now | 54
Thanks for waiting, Lord | 56
Accepting forgiveness | 58

Praise for Laughter | Backseat drivers | 62
Laughter and sorrow | 64
Childlike honesty | 66
No more social graces | 67

Prayers of
Thankfulness | Thanks for memories | 70
Thank you for prayer partners | 72
God's servants | 74
Thank you for lucid moments | 76
"Thanks for tears by now forgotten" | 78

Prayers That
Focus on Jesus | Yesterday, today, and forever | 82
Turning my eyes toward Jesus | 84
Becoming like a child | 85
Your example is for me, Lord | 86
A very special place | 88

PRAYERS ABOUT
STRENGTH AND HOPE   Streets of gold   *90*
                     Night thoughts   *92*
                     Reason to live   *94*
                     Enjoying God's fruit   *96*
                     Contagious hope   *98*
                     A lesson in hope   *100*
                     Time to let go   *102*

Optional Worship Helps for Caregiver and Care Receiver

                     Note to the Reader   *107*

PRAYERS FOR CARE
RECEIVERS   Praise God, who gives all good gifts   *110*
                     Forgive me, Lord   *111*
                     Prayer of thanks for wonderful memories   *112*
                     Prayer for God's mercy   *114*
                     Prayer of anticipation   *115*
                     Prayer for family and friends   *116*
                     The Lord's Prayer   *117*

PSALMS   Favorite passages from Psalm 1–150   *120*

OTHER
FAVORITE SCRIPTURES Verses from Proverbs to Malachi and
                     Matthew to Revelation   *140*

HYMNS AND
SPIRITUAL SONGS   Timeless favorites   *152*

INDEXES   *187*

Praying in Valleys and on Peaks: Prayers for Caregivers

N O T E   T O

THE READER

You, a loving caregiver, are often physically, emotionally, and mentally tired. Perhaps you are even spiritually drained sometimes. So you may find it difficult to compose prayers that express your true feelings to God. Because that has happened to me in the past, I would like to share with you some prayers that I have now been able to write.

I'm a single working woman who has cared for both of my parents. My father went to be with the Lord in July 1998; but as I write this book, my mother is still with me. You will learn a lot about our family as you read my prayers! Your situation may be like mine or very different from it. Whatever your experience has been or will be, it is my desire to help you express to God your honest thoughts and feelings. I want to help you talk with God about what you are currently facing as you care for a loved one.

After you read each prayer in this book, you'll have an opportunity to personalize it by reading through the application section. If you're not ready to share your own heart with God during the first reading, that's okay. Just mark the pages with prayers that most closely help you verbalize what you are going through at this time. Go back to those prayers and pray them again . . . and again . . . until you find yourself substituting or adding some of your own words.

I offer two prayers for each reader of this book. The first is that you will feel God's arms around you as you walk through the valleys. The second is that you will rejoice in knowing that God even now is leading you toward the peaks, no matter how far away they are.

Love in Christ,

Betty Free, caregiver to parents
Einar Free (November 1, 1903–July 17, 1998)
Helen Free (October 22, 1907–August 28, 2001)*

*Mom joined Dad in heaven during the time when editors, copy editors, and I were checking the typeset manuscript of this book. It happened on the night before her last caregiver left. (See "God's Perfect Timing," page 19.) On that night my mother quietly stopped breathing and walked right into heaven. Now she and my father are both with the best Caregiver of all!

Prayers of Adoration

The Lord's . . . compassions never fail. They are
new every morning; great is your faithfulness.

LAMENTATIONS 3:22-23, NIV

The one in charge

Dear Father in heaven,

How glad I am to be your child!
I'm also glad my parents taught me to depend on you,
    because as they grew older,
        I found myself calling on you for help more and
        more.

I praise you for being in charge of my dad's life
        from beginning to end, to glorious new
        beginning.
You brought Dad through cancer surgery and gave him
        almost twenty more years of life.
I praise you for being in charge of Mom's life too.
You brought her through chemotherapy twenty-five
        years ago, and she is still here!

You've been in charge all along, dear Lord.
    You've brought us through good and bad.
Now that Dad is with you and Mom at ninety-three
        is still with me,
    I'm glad you continue to be in charge.

I have many decisions to make about Mom's care.
And I need your help, dear Father.
    I must allow you to be the Lord of my choices.
Forgive me when I forget who is in charge.
    Help me not to try to do your work for you.

In the name of Jesus, my Lord and Savior.

Amen.

Sometimes it's difficult to allow God to be in charge—especially in tough situations. Even if you know God is in control, it's easy to think you need to handle things yourself. Ask God to help you trust him with the decisions in your life.

All I need to know

My faithful, loving, and merciful God,

I could never have made it
    to this point without you.

I praise you for never leaving me—
    even when I'm so busy that I don't realize how
        much I need to talk to you.
You have always been there for me,
    ready to comfort and help whenever I've kept my
        attention on you.

There are days I don't want to think about tomorrow.
Yet I know you'll be there for me tomorrow,
    just as you are here with me right now.

You've blessed me over and over again in ways I never
        anticipated.
So I do anticipate now, Lord, a blessed future.
    I must dream, Father, about a time when my load
        is lighter again.
    It will be. I know it will be.

In the meantime, you're here, Father.
    I praise you for being with me.
You'll never leave me,
    and that's all I need to know.

In the faithful, loving, and merciful
    name of Jesus I pray.

Amen.

Are you facing a difficult day? You might find it encouraging to praise God for some yesterdays when you could feel he was with you. Then dream about some pleasant tomorrows with your heavenly Father, and praise him for his faithful presence with you each day.

Dear God,

How I praise you for coming to earth in the person of Jesus Christ.

When you lived on earth, you didn't see crowds of people
        around you.
    You looked at individuals in the crowds and had
        compassion on them.
You saw a lame man, a sick girl, a grieving mother.

Now, as you look down from heaven, you don't see masses
        of humanity; you see individual people.
You see a frightened man in pain,
    a sad woman struggling to remember who she is,
    and a weary daughter doing her best to care for her parents.

I'm the weary daughter, and my friends try to understand
        what I'm going through.
    But they can't—not really.
My father was at one time the man in pain, and my mother is
        still the woman without a memory.
    I try to understand what they have been through.
    But I can't—not really.

" And he had

I praise you, God, for your compassion.
>You can understand everything—you really can!
As you look down from heaven, you see and understand
>>everything my family and I are facing.
>That's because on this earth you experienced pain,
>>rejection, sorrow, and weariness.

I thank you for understanding and caring.
>And I praise you for being the best Friend our family
>>ever had.
Your love and compassion never end.

Give me a measure of your compassion, Lord.
In your name I pray.

Amen.

ompassion on them "

How has Jesus shown compassion for you and your loved one?
Praise him for his love. In what ways would you like Jesus to help
you now? In what ways does your loved one need his compassion?
Ask the Lord for his touch on your home. Then go to sleep tonight,
resting in his loving, compassionate arms.

Now and forever

Father God,

I praise you for being my Father in heaven.
> You are so good to me.
Sometimes I wander away in my thoughts,
> in my words, or in my actions.
But like the father of the Prodigal Son, you're always
> waiting for me to come back.

Thank you, Father, for listening and opening
> your arms when I tell you how sorry I am.
Thank you for loving me even before I repent.
> And thanks for not shaking your finger at me
> because of my sins.

I praise you for offering me eternal life, Father God.
When I'm having a rough day with Mom,
> I think about what's ahead for her and me.
> Then the day goes by more quickly and
> with more hope.

Thank you that the eternal life you offer has already
> begun.
I'll talk to you every day, now and forever.
> Hallelujah!

Amen.

What do you need from your heavenly Father today? Do you need to feel his hand in yours? to accept his forgiveness? Maybe you long to thank him for caring for you as a father would. Why not tell him what you need today?

Prayers about Love and Family

God places the lonely in families.

Psalm 68:6

The gift of family

Heavenly Father,

I praise you for the gift of family.
When you created the world, you created birds,
        animals, and people to live in families.
You even created ants and bees to live and work
        together.

At the time of the Fall, people put a blemish on
        your creation of family, so human families
        are imperfect.
    But thank you for the gift of love, which can
        camouflage the imperfections.

There were just three of us in my family.
    Dad often referred to us as "we three Frees."
I praise you for the closeness our family shared.
    I praise you for selective memory, which blurs the
        pain of any negative times we experienced.
I praise you for giving me Christian parents,
    people who were committed to you and to helping
        their little girl grow up to follow you.

Our family has changed over the years.
    Now Mom and I are two.
We can't converse the way we once did, for Mom doesn't
        always hear or understand.
But the love is still there—for Dad, who is in heaven, and
        for Mom, who is sometimes Mom and sometimes
        my little girl.
Much of the time now Mom lives in a world of memories
        that go much farther back than "we three."

How I praise you for the day when Mom, even though
        she was uncertain about my identity, responded to
        my hug with these words:
    "I can't get things straight.
    But I know love and what it means."

Keep filling me with your love, Father.
Fill me so your love can flow through me to Mom.

In Jesus' loving name.

Amen.

Can you recall some good things about your family? You can praise God for happy times and at the same time ask him to blur any unhappy memories. Perhaps you'll find yourself wanting to jot a note to the loved one you care for, thanking this person for his or her love. You might even want to read your letter aloud to your loved one.

Total acceptance

Dear Lord,

How thankful I am that my parents loved me and
    understood me.
Just as you first loved me and gave me a desire to be like you,
    Lord, so Mom and Dad first loved me and made me
    want to be like them—loving, caring, and forgiving.
Over the years I've come to expect total acceptance
    from my family, as well as from you.

Father, I ask that you help me now when Mom
    becomes angry with me.
    Help me not to respond to anger with anger.
I know Mom isn't herself when she throws a tantrum.
    I know she is confused and frustrated and
    frightened.
What's my excuse, Lord?
    I still have the ability to reason and understand.
    Forgive me for expecting from Mom what she is
    no longer capable of giving.

Fill me with your love so that I can offer total
    acceptance even when it may seem undeserved.
    After all, my parents accepted me in spite of my
    faults, just as you do.
I need to pray the prayer of St. Francis of Assisi—
    especially the part that says, "Grant that I may
    not so much seek . . . to be understood
    as to understand."

In the name of my loving Savior.

Amen.

Prayer of St. Francis of Assisi

Lord,

Make me an instrument of your peace.
Where there is hatred, let me sow love;
where there is injury, pardon;
where there is doubt, faith;
where there is despair, hope;
where there is darkness, light; and
where there is sadness, joy.
O Divine Master,
grant that I may not so much seek
to be consoled as to console;
to be understood as to understand;
to be loved as to love.
For it is in giving that we receive;
it is in pardoning that we are pardoned;
and it is in dying that we are born to eternal life.

Did you feel totally accepted by your parents? Why or why not? Talk with God about your relationship with your family, thanking him for good relationships and asking for healing of memories where relationships were less than ideal.

Remember that God accepts you just as you are. Ask him to help you understand and accept the person you care for, even if that person is currently unable to understand or accept you.

Dear God,

I guess I'm a pretty typical caregiver.
    I'm a single daughter, working full-time.
        I'll soon be thinking about my own retirement.
    I have no siblings. (That may not be so typical.)
    Once in a while it would be very nice to have the
        input of a brother or sister.
    That's when I lean on Christian brothers and
        sisters, along with extended family.

Thank you, God, for providing my friend Dave to be
        there for me by phone every evening.
He gives wonderful advice and encouragement.
Thank you for my aunt and uncle, who check on me
        regularly, offering moral support and praying
        for Mom and me every day.
Thank you for my church family.
    They understand that my ability to serve is limited,
        and they take turns serving me instead.

Multiple

Lord, you know that married caregivers have additional
family responsibilities,
but you are capable of providing for their
needs just as you provide for mine.
Caregiving situations affect so many people, Lord.

I think about a married woman I know who stays
at home all day to care for a disabled child.
Another runs two households, caring for her own
family plus an elderly parent across town.
These women wouldn't survive, Lord, if their
husbands didn't offer a heap of love,
understanding, and assistance.
And the husbands wouldn't survive if they didn't
learn to accept the limitations on their wives'
time and energy.

I know children, grandchildren, and even nieces and
nephews who feel neglected and jealous,
the way they often do when a new baby arrives.
Lord, please help them and everyone else realize that
caregivers need extra love and understanding.

Amen.

relationships

Talk to God about your family relationships. Then sit down with a spouse, child, or other relative. Honestly discuss your needs and specific things this person could do to support you.

Also ask God to show you ways to find a little extra help so you can have a free afternoon or evening now and then to spend time with other family members.

Serving each other

Dear Lord,

I'm so glad for the many years you allowed my parents
   to have together.
They supported each other on the farm
   and showed their faithfulness to you in going
     to church together every Sunday.

What a sweet, helpful spirit you gave Dad during
   Mom's chemotherapy.
He took over grocery shopping and vacuuming and
   even became an expert dishwasher!

Then Mom returned the favor when Dad had cancer.
She waited on him "hand and foot," knowing he was
   too weak to do things for himself.
Sometimes she told me how tired she was.
   But you gave her strength to keep going.

Thank you for helping Mom and Dad to be content
   with the life you gave them,
  and for giving them a desire to serve each other.
Thank you for the example they set for younger
   couples—both in our church and in
   the community.
  And thank you for the blessing they were to me.

Amen.

If you are caring for a spouse, it may be difficult to relate to him or her in this new way. Why not talk together about how you both feel? One way to put each other at ease might be to find ways for your care receiver to serve you. Above all, ask God to be the center of this "new" relationship.

Still learning

Dear Lord,

As I have cared for Mom and Dad, I have learned
    so much from them—so much about you.

I learned from my dad's childlike faith that no matter
    how much we suffer in this life,
  there is no need to feel forsaken by you.
He showed me by his example that inner peace can
    overpower outward circumstances.
I also learned from my father that no matter how long
    someone has been a faithful Christian,
  it's important to ask daily for your forgiveness.

I'm learning from Mom that you always do forgive a
    repentant heart.
Sometimes I get impatient with Mom, and then she is
    aware of the burden she has become.
Then I look at Mom, my eyes filled with love for her and
    sorrow for my inconsiderate words.
I ask her to forgive me, and she does.
    She studies me carefully and says, "Oh, those eyes.
    Jesus understands, and he forgives you."
    She gives me a smile and a squeeze, and I feel
    clean and forgiven.

Thank you, heavenly Father, for godly parents,
    in whose footsteps I'm still seeking to follow.

Amen.

Make a mental or written list of ways the person you care for has been a good example. Offer your thanks to God and to your loved one for all you have learned from him or her. Then ask God to help the learning process continue.

An independent widow

Dear God,

I've been thinking about your care for one of my
    Sunday school teachers.
You graciously allowed her to live in her home until
    she was almost ninety years old.
You gave her the strength to work with Child
    Evangelism Fellowship and to deliver food
    and clothes to needy families.
But then she broke her hip, and suddenly she was
    receiving help instead of giving it.

Since she had always been so independent,
    her son needed help to know what to say
to keep his mother from feeling useless.
Thank you, Father, for the words you gave him:
    "Now you can be an example to older people.
    Show them that they can hang in there."

Is it hard for you to help your loved one feel needed? Ask God to show you some ways the person you care for can still minister to others. If he or she is able to stay in an assisted-living facility, thank God for the independence that allows.

Her son is thankful for the assisted-living facility
    his mother can live in.
You're using my teacher now, Lord, to minister
    to residents and staff there.
Her positive attitude and stories of God's provision
    over the years are an inspiration to everyone.

Thank you, Father, for helping this loving family
    adapt to a new situation,
    and for giving my teacher new ways to serve you.

Amen.

Prayers about Change

I am the Lord, and I do not change.

MALACHI 3:6

From kitchen to sofa

Dear Lord,

One evening a few years ago, Mom told me she had
    ruined one of her best pans.
She had forgotten that it was on the stove,
    and she let it run dry.
I've heard stories like that too often lately, Lord.
They used to happen to other people's mothers.
    Now they're happening to mine.

You gave Mom a love for the kitchen, Lord.
    In fact, it's always been her favorite room.
As a farmer's wife, she got up early each morning to
    bake a pie or cake for Dad and the hired man.

But the time came when Mom started spending more
    time on the sofa than in the kitchen.
She was tired a lot and couldn't remember things.
    Some of them were important things, like the fact
    that the stove was on.

Have you noticed changes in your loved one's actions? Bring the things you're concerned about to the Lord, asking him to show you how and when you should intervene.

It was time to get help for Mom in the daytime.
    And you knew just who she needed, Father.
    One of my prayer partners said, "Call Sharon."

Sharon, a nursing assistant, became like a daughter to
    my folks and a sister to me.
Thank you for her help when Mom needed more time
    on the sofa and less time in the kitchen.

Amen.

God's perfect timing

Oh, my Father, I don't know what to do. I depend so
    much on our nursing assistant, Sharon,
    who came when Mom's mind was still okay.
Mom knows her and trusts her.
    How can I find anyone to take Sharon's place now that
        she's retiring after three years with us?

Lord, it's been getting harder and harder to concentrate
        on my work at home.
    Mom requires more and more attention and care.
I think it's time for me to consider live-in help.
    That would give me the freedom I need
        to come and go, to keep the wonderful job
        you've given me.

～

Dear God, thank you for Josephine, who lived with
        Mom and me for over a year and shared your
        love with us.
Now a new caregiver is returning to her home after
        only two months.
Help me not to feel weary as I search for someone else
        to assist me with Mom's care.

Does God's timing sometimes seem wrong to you? Talk to him about your questions and frustrations. If you ask him, he'll help you trust him even before you understand.

Your timing is always right, dear Lord.
Thank you for knowing what's best for everyone
        long before we know or understand.
Help me to always trust you even before I understand.

Amen.

Dear Lord,

Thank you for the confidence I always had in the
     decisions my dad made.
You gave Dad a logical mind and a keen sense for
     good business dealings.
You know that Dad took care of his farming business
     without a lot of help from others.
    You gave him the ability to do math in his head
       more quickly and accurately than most people
       can do it on paper.

I was surprised when I discovered one day that Dad
     was having trouble balancing his checkbook.
Soon after that we learned Dad was losing his eyesight.
Lord, it was very difficult for my father to admit he
     couldn't handle his business affairs alone anymore.
But he did admit it . . . and eventually accepted it.

Dad gradually let me take over the checkbook.
He would sit by the kitchen table, listening as I told
     him how much the bills were and how much
     was left in his checking and savings accounts.

I'll take care

As time went on, Lord, Dad's interest in earthly
matters diminished, and his interest in heavenly
matters grew.
I'd tell him about a good deal and how much money I had
saved on a certain item, and Dad would say,
"Money isn't that important." And he was right.

Thank you for the gracious way my father allowed me
to take over his business affairs.
I'm glad, Lord, that you gave me a dad who taught me
to use common sense regarding money.
But I'm also glad you gave me a dad who knew
that money is not as important
as a right relationship with you.

In your name I pray.

Amen.

of that, Dad

As parents age, roles tend to reverse. What role reversals have you had in your family? It's not always easy for an older person to give up responsibilities, nor is it always easy for a spouse or child to take on additional responsibilities. Ask for God's help—and wisdom—in your situation.

Oh, Father in heaven,

Where did my sweet little mama go?
    Everyone used to say she was a very kind lady.
No one cared about other people more than she did.

Mama taught me never to say anything that might hurt
        someone else's feelings.
So I grew up to be a people lover like my mama.
But you know, Lord, that I've always had a spicier
        temperament than Mama had.

Now Mama is ninety-three.
Well, of course, you know that, Lord.
    You knew my mama long before I did.
    You formed her in Grandma's womb,
        and you know the number of days she has left.

When Mama's mind is working,
    she still is a loving, caring lady.
Why, Lord, doesn't her mind always work?
    Why does she get so angry?

Still my

Oh, Father, if Mama only knew how her words hurt—
    how they hurt me when she tells me,
        "There is no love in you."
    "Mama, I'm full of love—
        for Jesus, for you, for others."

Father God, thank you for the memories I have of Mama.
Thank you for helping me to keep on loving her even
        when she doesn't act loving toward me.
Forgive me for the times I have scolded her for not
        being kind.
For it's then that she cries and wants to be the sweet
        little mama she used to be.
    And yet that's what she still is.
        Don't let me ever forget it, Lord.

Amen.

sweet mama?

Has your loved one's personality changed? Or have there been other changes, perhaps in physical abilities and skills? Let God know how that makes you feel. Then thank him for the person your loved one used to be—and still is. You might want to display a photo that reminds you of the "real" personality that may often be hidden now.

Dear Lord,

It happened so quickly—the stroke that took away my
    mother's ability to talk and swallow.
Now I never know what she's saying,
    but I do know when Mom is angry and when she's
    happy.
I'm glad, oh Lord, there are different ways my mother
    can communicate her frustrations and joys.
I thank you for toothless smiles and wordless hugs.
    They show me that Mom can still have moments
        when she is filled with love and contentment.
I thank you for tears and sounds of lamentation.
    They show me she's also able to express her
        deepest feelings of anguish.

Lord, I had to make a decision following the stroke.
Would I still be able to keep Mom at home,
    or would I have to take her to a nursing home?
Would I allow a feeding tube or not?

It would have been easier if my parents had given me
    specific instructions about their last days.
    Instead they gave me power of attorney over health
    care and said, "You'll know what to do."

Home or

I'm pleased and honored that they trusted me.
But oh, dear God, how I've needed your wisdom!

After talking with the director of a hospice group,
I knew, Father, that you had led me to them.
They assured me they would keep Mom comfortable
and even hospitalize her as needed to relieve
symptoms that couldn't be treated at home.

I thank you for baby food and thickened juices that
Mom can swallow.
I thank you for our caregiver's patience as she feeds Mom
every couple of hours.

Lord, I know my mother's days on this side of eternity
are in your hands.
I ask you to be merciful to her—to take care of her,
comfort her, keep her close to you.
I love her, Lord, and I love you. Thank you for loving us.

Amen.

nursing home?

Has your loved one's health been changing? What decisions might you soon need to make? Ask God to give wisdom to you and mercy to your loved one. Then even now, in the midst of your worries, try to find at least one thing for which you can thank God.

Dear God,

I enjoy talking with my friend Marilyn, who took care
of her mother at home for nine years.
She and I can empathize with each other.

Thank you, Lord, for Marilyn's husband and family.
Her husband was the one who told his mother-in-
law she could live with them after her stroke.
One son gave up his bedroom, and the other two
often came home from high school at lunch to
check on Grandma while their mom was at work.

As time went on, Marilyn discovered that her mother's
mind was wandering more and more.
Then a fire took their home, their youngest son was
badly burned, and they moved into two apartments.
Marilyn knew the time had come—she could no longer
keep her mother at home.

Different

My friend's eyes fill with tears as she remembers
  taking her mother to a nursing home.
At first her mother was depressed and cried a lot.
  But then, Lord, you helped her find contentment.
  She learned to wheel herself to a Bible-study group,
    church services, and other activities.
  She even went out to lunch with friends.

Now Marilyn and her family bring Grandma home
  for Sunday dinners and family gatherings.
Marilyn realizes how much she resented having to
    center her life around her mother's needs for
    so many years.
  Now when Marilyn sees her mother after some downtime,
    she really *enjoys* her company.
My friend reminds me that choosing a nursing home is
    the right and loving decision for many caregivers.

Thank you, Father, for understanding the needs of caregivers
    and the needs of those we care for.
Thank you for allowing us to give our care in different
    ways and in different places at different times.

Amen.

Decisions

Do you feel tied down at times, not knowing how to escape from the caregiving responsibilities you've taken upon yourself? Then let God know what's difficult for you to handle right now, and ask him to show you changes you can make if it becomes necessary. Thank him for allowing you to be a caregiver—whether in your home or through regular visits with your loved one in a nursing facility.

The one constant in my life

I've had about all the change I can handle, Lord.
Dad has gone home to you.
Mom can no longer communicate except through
smiles and hugs—and temper tantrums.
And lately even *I* am facing new health problems.

But I have you, dear Lord.
You're the same as you've always been and the
same as you'll always be.
You will never move.
Your address will always be "Heaven."
I can count on you to be there for me.
You will always hear me and understand me.
You will always love me and care for me.

Thank you, Father God, for being the one constant
in my life.
I'm learning to accept the changes you send my way
because I know *you* won't change—not ever.
I've also discovered that good, unexpected things often
follow the changes you send.

I can see you at work, Lord, especially when I face
changes I'd rather not have to deal with.
Thank you for being in control of all the changes
in my life.
When I look around the corner to see what's next, I see
that you're already there waiting for me.
Thank you, God.

Amen.

What changes in the last few years have been particularly difficult? Can you name one good outcome of each change? No matter what's changing in your life, God stays with you. Thank him for that, and ask him to help you accept any changes you're struggling with right now.

Prayers about Worries and Fears

Look at the lilies and how they grow. . . . If God cares
so wonderfully for flowers that are here today and
gone tomorrow, won't he more surely care for you?

MATTHEW 6:28, 30

Dear Father,

I just had a little pain in my neck and shoulder.
  But right away my doctor used the *D* word.
  You know which one I mean, Lord—*degenerative.*
"Doctor, you've got to be kidding!" I said.
  "Mom is the one who is degenerating.
  She's in her nineties. I'm only sixty."
  My doctor wasn't impressed. "It happens," he said.

And then my doctor read the results of my blood test.
  Right away he used one of the *C* words.
  You know that word too, Lord—*cholesterol.*
"I've really been trying to watch what I eat," I said.
  "Mom's cholesterol is normal. Why is mine high?"
"Many factors are involved," said my doctor.
  "Try these pill samples. You need help."

He's got that right, Lord.
  I need help, but I need more than pills.
I need help to believe that you, Father, will see me
    through the changes that occur in my own life.
  I have watched you care for my folks.
  I must trust you to care for me as well.

facing my

I don't have children to look after me, Lord.
My friend Dave, who lives two thousand miles away,
doesn't have children either.
But we've had fulfilling lives, serving you as singles.
I pray that you'll help both of us make wise plans for
our futures.
We each need to think about what we will do for
long-term care if it should be needed.
But more important than that, help us to find ways to
serve you as long as we live, wherever we live.

I'm facing some changes that sound frightening,
Lord.
Others sound wonderful.
Thank you that you have me in your hands,
no matter what retirement brings.

In Jesus' name.

Amen.

own changes

What changes are occurring in your life right now? Health problems? Others? Why not talk to God about your concerns and fears, asking him to help you trust him for your future. He may plant long-range ideas in your mind for things you can do for him—and for yourself—when you're no longer a caregiver. And other ideas, short-range, that you can do right now to give yourself a break!

After Dad turned ninety, he figured he had lived
        long enough, Lord.
"I'm too old," he'd often say, smiling.

Dad trusted you like a child does, Father—he had
                few worries or fears.
        But he didn't want to be a burden to anyone,
                and he didn't want to outlive his money.

I made sure he never felt like a burden, dear God.
        And I know he didn't outlive his money.
So the only two things he feared never happened.

Mom, on the other hand, has always worried about
                everything.
        She knew she should have trusted you more, Lord.
She often felt bad that she didn't.
        Now her mind seldom works right.
Sometimes she smiles like a contented baby.
        But much of the time her brow is wrinkled as she
                tries to understand what she's worried about
                and why.

No more

I'd like to help Mom worry less.
Yet all I can do is smile at her, hug her, and tell her
over and over again that everything is all right.
I pray for her and tell her that I love her.
I tell her you love her too, because you do.
I keep trying, and sometimes I get a slight smile.
So thank you, Lord, for helping Mom worry less.

But most of all, Lord, I thank you that Dad is with
you in the "land of no fear."
One day Mom will be there with him, completely
fearless for the first time in her life.
And I'll rejoice that I need have no worries or fears as
I continue my own journey home.

Amen.

worries

*Does your loved one have worries or fears? What about you? Tell
God about your situation and turn all your concerns over to him.
He can take care of them—and you can be assured that he will!*

Carefree Days

Dear God,

Sometimes I like to sit back and remember when I was
   a little girl and didn't have a care in the world.
That's a few years ago, God, but I still remember life
   on the farm.
   It was a secure place where everyone was always busy,
      always accepted, always loved.

I remember playing hide-and-seek with Snuggie Bug,
   my very first dog.
   He was just a mutt—mostly rat terrier—but that
      didn't matter to me.
   With no siblings and no close neighbors, he kept
      me from being lonely.
   Thank you, Lord, for memories of Snuggie Bug.

When I was eight, you helped Mom and Dad find a
   farm they could purchase for themselves.
   After we moved to the new farm, I went to a
      different school and met a girl named Margie.
   She and I became very good friends and spent
      many happy hours playing together.
   Thank you, Lord, for memories of Margie.

Then there was Leslie, the young man who came to
      work for my dad and who lived with us for
      seven years.
You knew Dad needed a cheerful, hard worker to keep
      his spirits up when he grew weary.
And you knew I needed a "big brother" who would
      remain part of the family over the years.
Thank you, Lord, for memories of Leslie.

Now I have so many decisions to make every day, and
      I feel so tired when Mom keeps me awake at night.
I dread the days when I have to be alone with Mom
      and she is agitated, unable to think logically.
I try to keep her as calm and as happy as I can, but
      often there's nothing I can do to help her.
On those days I am especially thankful to you, Lord,
      for memories of carefree days, now long gone.

In Jesus' precious, loving name I pray.

Amen.

Are your days filled with decisions you need to make and problems that seem impossible to solve? Look for moments when you can let your mind wander back to carefree days. As you thank God for the comfort those memories bring, you'll discover he is still with you and able to help you cope with today's cares.

Dear heavenly Father,

I know you are a God of mercy and love.
And I know you care for me even more than my earthly
    parents did.

I also know you have cared for Mom and Dad all
    through their emotionally and physically
    difficult times.
    They have always trusted you, Lord.
Dad had a childlike faith that sustained him through
    prostate cancer and almost total blindness.
Mom trusted you through chemotherapy, which—
    along with the prayers of your people—took
    lymphoma from her body over twenty-five
    years ago.

But in their last years Dad suffered from pain, and
    dementia took its toll on Mom.
Irrational fears set in—some brought on by the pain or
    the dementia, some perhaps caused by
    medications.
    "Don't leave me alone," Dad would say.
    "I don't know where I'm at," Mom would
    complain.

No

Lord, I see no reason for those irrational fears.
> Only you know why you allowed them to come.

Maybe you wanted me to learn how to comfort my
> parents.

Perhaps you wanted them to be willing to let go of this
> life and yearn more for the next.

Father, I know people who *should* have fears.

They are the people who don't know you.

They don't realize that they are not ready to enter the
> kingdom of heaven.
>> I pray for them, Lord.
>> I pray you will open their eyes.

Create a healthy fear in their hearts that will lead them
> to your perfect love and to an eternity where no one will
> have any fears.

In the name of Jesus, my Savior, I pray.

Amen.

reason

Is your loved one experiencing irrational fears? If you talk about this with God, he may give you songs of assurance and Scriptures such as Psalm 23 to share. If your loved one isn't a Christian, the Holy Spirit may bring passages to your mind to repeat often. You might read verses such as John 1:12 and Romans 10:9 and then talk to your loved one about accepting Christ.

It's your money, God

Dear heavenly Father,

When there is so much to think about as I try to survive each day, I really don't like having to think about money, too.
You know that right now most of my take-home pay goes to Mom's live-in caregiver.

We have Mom's Social Security check, along with some interest from investments for other expenses.
So far we've been able to stay in our house.
So far I've been able to continue supporting my missionary friends and my "child" in Colombia.

You've provided the extra income I've needed to keep going this year, but thinking about next year sometimes makes me anxious.

Do you have financial concerns? Ask God to direct you to people who can give you good advice. Then make plans for the future and trust God to intervene if he has better plans for you.

My car has passed the one-hundred-thousand-mile mark, and the transmission is whining.
But I can't afford a new car right now, so I ask you, Lord, to keep this one running.

I need your wisdom as I plan how to use our money.
I realize it's really not Mom's money or mine.
It's your money, God.
Thanks for helping me use it wisely.
Thanks for caring for Mom and me even more than you care for birds and lilies.

In Jesus' name I pray, with thanksgiving.

Amen.

Prayers about Pain and Suffering

I heard a loud voice from the throne saying, "Now the dwelling of God is with men, and he will live with them. They will be his people. . . . He will wipe every tear from their eyes. There will be no more death or mourning or crying or pain."

REVELATION 21:3-4, NIV

Dear Lord,

When I was a little girl and got "owies," Mom always
       knew how to fix them.
Whenever I was worried about something, Dad knew
       how to calm my jittery nerves.
Between the two of them, my parents could fix just
       about anything.

I'm so grateful to you, Father God, for your provision.
But oh, Lord, how sad I feel when I can't repay Mom
       and Dad by fixing things for them.

When they were in their seventies and eighties,
       I could take them to the doctor, discuss their
              symptoms, and get the help they needed.
But after they turned ninety, the fix-it well began
       to run dry.

I can't fix

Dad was in so much pain before he died.
　　The medicine that had once worked was no longer
　　　　effective,
　　and I couldn't fix things for him.
After Mom had the stroke that left her unable to talk,
　　I couldn't fix that either, God.
A couple of years earlier she'd said to Christmas guests,
　　"If you couldn't talk to people, you'd just wilt."
Oh, Father, I cry when I recall those words.

Mom sits in her wheelchair now, sometimes smiling,
　　　　sometimes with a blank expression, but never
　　　　able to say anything.
She rambles on and on, offering an array
　　of nonsense syllables.
Maybe that's how you help her keep from wilting, Lord.

Help her, Jesus, to cope, because I can't fix things anymore.

Amen.

it anymore

What are some things you wish you could fix for your loved one? Talk to God about them, and tell him how much it hurts when you can't fix it anymore. He already knows, but he waits for you to bring your burden to him so he can comfort you.

Dear Father in heaven,

You gave me a mother who was bright and full
        of common sense.
Although not a teacher by profession, she was the one
        who taught me to read.
She even showed me how to write my name when
        I was four.
Now, Lord, the wonderful mother you gave me
        struggles to remember who she is.

I recall the morning Mom started calling out numbers.
She sat in her wheelchair by the breakfast table, her
        eyes tightly closed as she began counting:
    "One, two, three, four, seven, six, eleven, twelve,
        thirteen . . . fourteen!"
She drank some coffee.
    "Now I'm all confused. . . . 166, 167 . . . I don't
        know where I'm at."
    Then she looked at me and asked, "Did I disappoint
        you? I'm so slow."

Making sense

I told her that when you're ninety-two it's all right
      to be slow.
   Thank you for giving me those words of reassurance
      for her.
Mother smiled and looked relieved. "Oh, good."
She opened her eyes and added, "I'll try to be a little
      bit sensible."

Later that morning my mother talked to you, God.
   She said, "I have suffered so, Father.
      I can't suffer anymore. Come, dear Jesus.
      Come stay with us."
   She *has* suffered more since then, Lord.
      But you have stayed with us.
Thank you for your presence and the comfort
      it brings.

Amen.

of it all

Has your loved one experienced mental anguish? Pray that you will become more aware of the Lord's comforting presence. You can be assured that he'll bring you and your loved one through this valley, just as he has brought you through every other valley.

Dear heavenly Father,

One morning several years ago Mom woke up unable
    to say anything but nonsense words.
      After an hour, when she was able to speak again,
      she said, "I'm in a different world."
She hummed "Jesus, Keep Me Near the Cross."
    My voice cracked, Lord, as I sang the chorus:
    "In the cross, in the cross be my glory ever
    Till my raptured soul shall find rest beyond the river."

Mom's speech was garbled off and on that day.
    After I put her to bed, she hummed this song:
      "Jesus calls us; o'er the tumult
      Of our life's wild, restless sea,
      Day by day His sweet voice soundeth,
      Saying, 'Christian, follow Me.'"

The next morning I felt sad, dear Father,
    when Mom had to ask if she was my mother.
"For a while I thought I wasn't," she said.
    "I was a little insane, you know."
I felt sad again when Mom commented,
    "It's like I've lost something—I guess I have."

Jesus by

But oh, heavenly Father, how my spirits lifted as Mom
    shared these spiritual insights:
"When things aren't as they should be, it's wonderful
    to come to Jesus.
    He takes your hand and forgives you.
There are things that keep us from thinking just right,
    but he says, 'I forgive you,' and he gives his peace.
        It's no one's fault.
    Sometimes I think it's my fault, but I'm wrong.
I'm so hungry for Jesus. I love my Jesus so much.
Come, Jesus, help me feel your presence.
    Help Betty feel it too."

And Lord, I do feel I'm in your presence when Mom
    talks so naturally with you.
She may be going downhill physically and mentally,
    but spiritually she's rising all the way.
    Thank you for letting me be part of the journey.

Amen.

your side

*If your loved one is experiencing mental or physical difficulties, ask
God to help you see positive changes that may be taking place spiritually. And whenever your loved one shows signs of joy in God's
presence, praise God for this encouragement.*

Dear God,

I know there's a spiritual war going on all around us.
I've been very aware of it as I've watched my parents
      sit on the edge of this life, waiting to step
      into eternity.

Dad, who was always the ultimate optimist, began to question
      your love when his physical heart kept beating but his
      spiritual heart yearned for heaven.
    He would ask, "Doesn't God forgive my sins?
      Doesn't he love me anymore? Why won't he
      take me home?"
    I had no answers except to say that your timing is
      perfect, God, even when your answers to our
      prayers come more slowly than we'd like.

Mom, who always wanted to live long so she could help
      others, now lives only because others help her.
    This wiry little woman now waits for you to
      take her home, Lord.

Doesn't God

I wonder: Does Satan take advantage of the final
    months with God's children, doing whatever he
    can to make them miserable?
    He knows it's his last chance.
I thank you that my parents never gave up believing
    in you.
    They knew you would someday welcome them to
    heaven, even though sometimes they wished
    that day would come sooner.

Lord, be with Mom as she awaits her final move.
    Her bags are packed, and she's ready.
I've told her to follow you, her Shepherd, wherever
    you lead her.
    I've told her it's okay.
We'll wait patiently, Lord, for you to give Mom the
    final desire of her heart.

Amen.

love me anymore?

Have you talked to God about your loved one's spiritual questioning and suffering? God may lead you to a passage such as Romans 8 that you can read together. Seek protection under God's wings so the effects of Satan's attempts to create misery are minimized.

Dear Lord,

Ever since I was five, you and I have walked together.
   Now, for several years, we've been traveling
      through a valley.

When my folks first became totally dependent on me,
      I actually enjoyed my new mothering role.
Because I'm single, I had never experienced what
      people sometimes refer to as "the joys
      of motherhood."
   But when Dad could no longer dress himself, it was
      a *joy* to help him and to rub noses as I buttoned
      his shirt!
   Then as Mom became fearful and needed help
      making decisions, it was a *joy* to hold, comfort,
      and advise my "little girl."

In the

But then, Lord, it became difficult for Dad to cope with pain.
That was not a joy to watch, but I'm glad I
was there.
I was able to suffer with him, to get the best
medical help I could, to pray for him, and
to seek the prayers of family and friends.
Dad has gone to heaven—he couldn't be in
a better place!
The tears still come, but I know he is safe with you.

Now I watch Mom drool and pick at her skirt all day long
since she had her last stroke.
That gives me no joy, God.
I wish Mom could talk, but she can't.

We're going to be in the valley a while longer, Lord,
but I know you will bring the distant peaks into focus
in your own good and perfect time.
Keep me going till then, heavenly Father.
Hold my hand, and—oh, yes—please don't let go
of Mom's hand either.

Amen.

valley

What emotional valleys have you been traveling through? Is it difficult to believe there are peaks ahead? If you reach out for God's hand, you'll find he is right there beside you. And if you thank God for what he's helping you do now, you'll be able to trust him for what he has ahead for you.

Fourteen years of care

Dear Lord,

My experience with Mom and Dad seems short when
I think about a man who suffered for
fourteen years with multiple sclerosis.
During all of that time he and his wife had a caregiver
living with them.

It was good to talk with his wife, Lord.
She helped me realize that I'm not the only one
going through difficult times.
She told me she had a different caregiver almost every
year, some of whom were acceptable and
some of whom were not.

Father, I appreciated hearing about the help this
woman received from hospice.
The nurse carefully described what to expect at
the end and patiently explained to the
caregiver what he would need to do.
She offered morphine, which could be given to ease
breathing and pain.

Lord, what a beautiful transition from this life to the
next this family provided for their husband
and father as they sang, prayed, and read
Scripture together.
Thank you that you gave them this closure.

In the holy name of your Son, Jesus.

Amen.

Difficult caregiving situations can seem never-ending. If you tell God how you feel, perhaps he will help you find another caregiver with whom you can spend some time chatting. Sharing experiences can ease the grief that accompanies a loved one's transition from this life to the next.

Prayers for Forgiveness

When you are praying, first forgive anyone you are holding a grudge

against, so that your Father in heaven will forgive your sins, too.

MARK 11:25

If we confess our sins to him, he is faithful and just to forgive us

and to cleanse us from every wrong.

1 JOHN 1:9

Dear God,

Sometimes life just doesn't seem fair,
    and I stomp my foot.
Sometimes I get upset when I think about how much
        my folks have suffered,
    and I ask, "Why, why, why?"
Sometimes I think I can't handle Mom's insane
        behavior any longer,
    and I scream when I get in the car.

Lord, I'm glad I can express my feelings to you
        and know that you understand.
Thank you for listening to my questions.
    Help me to really believe you're there so I'll listen
        for your answers.

You're the potter, God.
    My parents are clay, and I'm clay.
        Forgive me for doubting that you have a purpose for
            the reshaping we have felt
        and the firing we've experienced in the kiln.
Thank you for being a merciful potter.

It's not

On the other hand, Father God, I know that not
      everything that happens in this world
   is the result of your potter's wheel.
In our fallen world, life is not always fair.
    Forgive me for contributing to this world's sinfulness.
    Make me your obedient and thankful child,
      trusting you to care for my parents and me as we
       travel in this foreign land.

Thank you for glimpses in your Word of our final destination.
I'm glad the *eternal* life you give won't be fair either,
    for we won't receive the condemnation we deserve.
We'll receive the life you bought for us at the cross.

With thanksgiving I pray in the name of Jesus.

Amen.

fair, God!

Are you angry about situations in your life that seem unfair? Express
your feelings honestly to God, who understands. His Son's death on a
cross wasn't fair, but he was willing to let it happen for our sake.

   It's okay to ask questions. But if you've been using them as a
reason to doubt God and his sovereignty, confess that to him. Then
ask him to help you trust him for the future.

Dear Father in heaven,

Help me not to feel bitter toward people who have
        stopped being involved in my parents' lives.
I have made the choice to see my parents through
        to their graduation from this life.
    After all, they saw me through
        to my graduation from childhood.
Almost everyone has supported me in this effort, but a
        few have become noticeably absent.

I still remember the first year when my parents and I
        were not invited to a small family Christmas
        celebration.
    I felt so sad as I listened to Mom and Dad express
        how unloved they felt.
    I've been upset about that incident for a long time.
        Forgive me, Lord. Help me to let it go.

Times are

My parents used to be a very hospitable couple.
  Every feed salesman, repairman, pastor, and
      neighbor who came to the farm was offered
      coffee and Swedish breads, cookies, or other pastries.
Times are different now.
  Most people don't just drop in to say hi anymore.
And, of course, we can't offer the conversations or the
      goodies that used to be a part of our daily lives.
Help me not to feel lonely when days and weeks go by
      without any visitors.

Thank you for those who do drop in unexpectedly for a
      ten-minute visit.
  What a joy it always is when girls from the church
      come to play their current piano pieces for us.
  What a pleasant surprise when former neighbors
      are in the area and come to say hello.
Show me how to let others know that casual, short,
      drop-in visits are welcome.
And thanks for being our perfect Guest every day.

  Amen.

Different now

Are you holding a grudge against anyone you feel has forsaken you, leaving you alone with your loved one? Perhaps it's a sibling who lives far away or a friend who no longer comes to visit. Ask God to help you let it go. He can help point you to someone who will listen to you, understand your situation, and help you not feel so alone.

Dear God,

My days often seem like a blur.
　　There is always something to do.
　　There is never time to think.
Forgive me, Lord, for bypassing you when I'm
　　　hurrying from home to work to the grocery store
　　　to the mall and, yes, even to church.
My intentions are good, but forgive me, Lord, for the
　　　many times I fail to carry out those intentions.

I'm glad, heavenly Father, that you hear me when I cry
　　　out to you along the way:
　　when I'm getting ready for the day,
　　when I'm trying to cope with an unpleasant
　　　situation with Mom,
　　when I'm driving somewhere—anywhere.
But oh, Lord God, please help me to be more
　　　intentional about my good intentions.

Thanks for

I love you, God, and I couldn't survive without your love.
Thank you for caring about me and understanding me.
Thank you for patiently waiting for me to come to you:
waiting to comfort me
when I'm feeling sorry for myself,
waiting to offer me your wisdom
when I'm trusting in my own knowledge,
waiting to give me strength
when my fuel gauge is registering "empty."

Thank you for this time with you, Lord.
It is always good to come into your presence,
acknowledging that you are God,
and Mom and I are the sheep of your pasture.
I praise you for who you are.
I thank you for being good.
Your love and faithfulness will continue forever.

Amen.

waiting, Lord

Is it hard for you to find time to talk to God? Seek his forgiveness and thank him for understanding that your regular devotional time may not be as regular as it once was. Perhaps one way you can spend time with God is to read Scripture passages to your loved one and sing songs with him or her. See the "Optional Worship Helps" section at the back of this book for some ideas.

Dear God,

As I was growing up, my parents and I took seriously
    Paul's advice to the Ephesians about anger.
We seldom let the sun go down without telling each
    other we were sorry for any thoughtless words
    spoken or hurtful actions committed on that day.

There's no doubt that Paul was inspired by your Holy
    Spirit to give that advice.
It's so much wiser than the line from an old movie
    called *Love Story* that said, "Love is never
    having to say you're sorry."
How presumptuous! How arrogant!
    Who but you, God, has the right to say that?
    Who but you can so perfectly express your love
    that you never have to say you're sorry?

Accepting

Now, Lord, I still tell Mom I'm sorry when I've been thoughtless.
  Sometimes she is able to smile and hug me to show
    her forgiveness.
  But more often she is unresponsive, sitting in her
    wheelchair with her mouth hanging open.
Those are difficult times for me, Lord.

I'm thankful that I have a live-in caregiver's help now.
  That gives me time to get more rest than I did for a while.
So I don't get upset with Mom as much as I once did,
  and I don't have to offer apologies as often now.

But when I need forgiveness, I continue to tell Mom, who
    I'm sure understands more than I realize.
  And I tell you, because I need your perfect love and
    your total forgiveness.

In the name of your Son, Jesus, who died for me
  so that I can be forgiven of all sin.

Amen.

forgiveness

Are there episodes with the person you care for—either ancient history or current events—that make you feel guilty? Your loved one may or may not express forgiveness. But confess sinful actions or words to your loved one, as well as to God. Whether or not you receive a verbal response from the person you care for, you can know that God understands and will honor your confession.

Praise for Laughter

There is a time for everything, and a season for every activity

under heaven: a time to weep and a time to laugh.

ECCLESIASTES 3:1, 4, NIV

Dear God,

You allowed Dad, Mom, and me to have some
        delightful vacations together.
Thanks, God, for each special experience.

When we traveled by car, Dad did the driving,
    I did the navigating, and Mom did the worrying!
We laughed, sang, talked, took pictures, and ate in
        restaurants with good home cooking.

After Dad became legally blind, we still traveled.
But Mom drove only to familiar places near home,
    so I had to do all of the driving on long trips, and
        you knew that wasn't safe, Lord.
I was ready to give up vacations—then you sent an
        old friend, Dave.
        Thank you for bringing our families together again.

Long ago Dave's father and mine had been best friends.
    Our mothers had also been friends.
How exciting it was to have Dave join us on a trip from
        our home in the Chicago area to New England!

Backseat

Dave and I still talk about that trip, Lord.
We laugh as we recall the backseat drivers who appeared
        to have even more fun on the trip than we did.
We get a bit hysterical when we recall the day I was
        trying to get to a little town in Vermont before dark.
    As I drove along a hilly, curvy, two-lane road under
        construction I heard Dad say, "Slow down!"
    "Be careful. I can't take this anymore!" said Mom.
        "Okay, okay!" I said.
    Dave just looked at me and smiled.

I'm glad, Lord, that when I'm feeling sad, Dave and
        I can still recall that drive and laugh about it.
Thanks for the soul medicine that needs no
        prescription.

Amen.

drivers

Can you recall some special experiences you have had with the person you're caring for? Spend some time reminiscing with your loved one about the fun times you've had. Tell God how much you enjoyed those times together, and talk to him about funny things that make you laugh.

Dear God,

There are days when I could be overcome with sorrow
        because life is so difficult for Mom.
But I know you don't want me to feel so sad that I'm
            unable to give Mom a smile,
        so I try not to dwell on the things she and my dad
            have had to go through mentally and physically.

Thank you, Lord, for the cute things Mom said during
        the time when she could still talk but her mind wasn't
        functioning just right.
Recalling Mom's humorous words helps me remember
        how she used to enjoy making people laugh.

When Mom wanted to help me dry dishes one evening,
        her mind couldn't tell her how to move her wheelchair.
But her words told me, Lord, that the mind you gave her
        was still at work.
    We laughed together when she said, "My feet can't think,
        so I can't come to you!"

Laughter

Then there was the night, Father, when Mom was
    awake every hour.
    Actually, there have been a number of nights like that,
    but not too many, for which I thank you.
I finally said to Mom, "Please be quiet and go to sleep."
    Not to be "out-mothered" by me, she said, "You
    behave too!"
    At three in the morning I wasn't laughing, but now
    I can look back at the incident and laugh.
    Thanks for helping me do that, Lord.

One day Mom asked me how old she was.
    I told her she was almost ninety-three.
"That's too old," said Mom. "You'll have to do the living
    for me."
    Yes, Lord, I do much of Mom's living for her now.
    As I do, thank you for giving me laughter amid
    the sorrow.

Amen.

If you feel so tired and burdened that it's difficult to laugh, ask God to help you look for the humor in situations you encounter today and in the week ahead. As you allow yourself to laugh, thank God for helping you do it.

Childlike honesty

Dear Lord, I'm so glad people understand that
      Mom doesn't always mean what she says.
And they know she isn't always able to say
      what she means.
Then again, often she is as honest and innocent
      as a preschooler, saying exactly what
      she means!

Sometimes I still think about Laura, God.
      She was the part-time caregiver Mom said was
      too bossy.
Mom told Laura, "You think you're the Big Cheese,
      but it doesn't work that way."
Then Mom told me, "I shouldn't have said that.
      I'd better buy Laura a box of candy!"

Father, sometimes I feel like telling people exactly
      what I think.
But I'm not in my nineties, so it wouldn't sound cute
      if it came from me.
There are times when Mom's words don't sound so
      cute either.
      When she embarrasses me, give me the grace
      to smile.
Help me to quietly remind the offended person how
      appalled Mom would be if she understood
      what she just said.
      I thank you that Mom herself often shows regret
      for words that are more hurtful than funny.

Amen.

Have you ever been embarrassed by the childlike honesty of your loved one? Rather than scolding or reacting with anger, ask God to help you rehearse ways to deal with the situation quietly and lovingly the next time your loved one displays a lack of tact.

No more social graces

Father in heaven, you are the best Father.
I'm glad you are so understanding.
    You understand me,
    you understand Mom,
        and you accept us both all the time.

Mom threw a temper tantrum one night,
    shaking her fists at caregiver Julie.
Oh, how I thank you for Julie,
    who just laughed about it.
After Julie put her to bed,
        Mom began to apologize
            for the way she had acted.
        "I didn't mean it,"
            she said remorsefully.
    Then she thought for a minute and said,
        "Well, maybe I did!"
Julie and I laughed uncontrollably.
    Mom looked at us and began laughing too.

Thank you, Father,
    for helping us see the humor.
    Thank you for showing me I can relax
        and not feel uptight when Mom's social graces
        fly out the window.

Amen.

Have you been feeling uptight lately? Ask God to send a friend who can help you see the lighter side. When you find yourself relaxing enough to laugh with your loved one, thank God! Be joyful about every smile that crosses his or her face.

Prayers of Thankfulness

Tell God what you need, and thank him for all he has done.
If you do this, you will experience God's peace, which is far
more wonderful than the human mind can understand.

PHILIPPIANS 4:6-7

Dear Lord,

The Swedish hymn "Thanks to God for My Redeemer"
        reminds me of many things for which to thank you.
When days and nights are long, it is sometimes difficult
        to feel like saying prayers of thanks.
    But if I pray as the hymn says—"Thanks for times now
        but a memory"—I begin to experience your
        peace and contentment.

Father, first I want to thank you for memory itself.
You created us with the ability not only to enjoy life
        together as a family,
    but also to enjoy remembering over and over again
        the many good times we have had.

Then, Lord, I want to thank you for some of the family
memories that are special to me.
Thanks for Sunday afternoon rides, for Christmas Eve suppers
around a candlelit table, and for birthday parties with
Grandma Ross, aunts, and uncles.
Thanks for spontaneous day trips, planned vacations, and
evening escapades in search of butterscotch ripple
ice cream cones and root-beer floats.

And I thank you for the many times Mom and Dad sacrificed
their time and energy to care for me.
Thanks for the times when Dad put aside precious moments
in the fields to go into town and pick up medicine for
my strep throat or bronchitis.
Thanks, Lord, for the many hours Mom spent caring for me
when I had rheumatic fever.

Thanks, too, for ordinary evenings.
We enjoyed family TV programs and played games.
We also read the Bible and prayed together.

With thanksgiving for all of this and more I pray.

Amen.

for memories

What are some happy times with family that are now only memories for you? As you care for your loved one, you might enjoy talking about some of those times and thanking God for each of them. Being able to remember those special times is also a gift—thank God for that, too!

Lord, how I thank you for prayer support.
   It has helped to see me through crises and has sustained
      me during long, mundane days.

Thank you for the pastor who said, when Mom had cancer,
      "Let us have faith for you."
Thank you for the four men who anointed Mom with oil.
      It was as if they let her down through the roof
         to Jesus.
      After they left, Mom thought someone was still
         in the house, for she felt your presence, Father.

Thank you for the woman at church who puts together
      the prayer chain.
   We have shared many prayers together.
Thanks for aunts, uncles, and cousins who have
      remembered our family over the years.
   We pray for them every day too.

Thank you, God, for one of my coworkers, who "just
      happens" to stop by my office whenever I'm in
      need of special prayer.
   She is so in tune to your Spirit—thank you for her.

Thank you

Thank you for good friends who always tell me they are
      praying for me.
I know that when they promise to pray, they do.
I thank you for the power that their prayers have
      had in my life and in the lives of my parents.

Lord, so many people have told me they don't understand
      how I can be so strong.
I know it's you, God, who has kept me healthy
      through all the years I've been caring for my folks.
You have given me wisdom along the way.
You have provided the energy I need.
And even though there have been some "down" days,
      you have seen me through those times.

Thank you, heavenly Father, that you never tire of hearing
      and answering prayer.
Thank you for those who never tire of praying.

Amen.

for prayer partners

Who supports you in prayer? Thank God for these people, and let them know how much their prayers mean to you. Perhaps you need prayer partners. Let your pastor or a friend know about your need, and pray that God would supply the right people to encourage you through prayer.

Father, I know you send to each congregation
the people who are needed to serve you at any
given time.
I have experienced this time and again as members
of my church family have met my needs
as a caregiver.

Thank you for so many friends who have ungrudgingly
stayed with Mom and Dad so I could run errands.
Thank you for the evenings when a young man from
church came to sing, giving my folks a private
concert.

When Dad needed shots for pain, a registered nurse
from our congregation lived nearby.
She came over twice every day for several weeks to
administer the shots.
Thank you for her "I-can-handle-it; it's-okay"
attitude that helped to keep us calm.

God's

The nurse and her husband were both there for us many times.
When our dog developed inoperable cancer, they took care
of the dog and buried him for me.
Before I learned how to pivot Mom from recliner
to wheelchair, this couple came more than once
to get Mom up from the floor!
Thank you, Lord, for these friends.

Thank you for the three families who surprised me on my
birthday one month after Dad died.

Thank you for the mother with two teenagers who said
on Christmas Eve, "We're coming for coffee and
bringing cookies. When should we come?"
Mom passed the cookies over and over again, and they
dutifully took one each time!
I survived the first Christmas Eve without Dad because
you sent us this family, Father.

Thank you for showing your love through the volunteer
help of so many people.

In the loving name of Jesus I pray.

Amen.

servants

Can you think of times when neighbors, friends, church family members, or relatives have met your needs? Thank God for each of these people.

If you need volunteer help, check with your church, a senior services office, a social worker at a local hospital, or a hospice group. There are people out there who can give you the help you need—ask God to match you up with the right ones.

Dear God,

I thank you for the wonderful mother you gave to me.
It's hard when I can't find my mother anymore.
   She hides behind the dementia that has erased
      reality.
   She hides behind the silence of a stroke that has left
      her unable to speak.
   She hides behind the anger that lashes out when she
      can't make sense of the world around her.

Most of the time, Father God, I feel like a motherless child,
      even when my mother is sitting right beside me.
   She stares out the window or plays with her
      stuffed animals.
   She hardly ever looks at me when I talk to her.

Thank you

But oh, Lord, how wonderful it is when I walk over
   to Mom and a big smile spreads across her face!
I tell her I need a hug, and she gives me one.
   It's a special mother-daughter hug that feels
   so wonderful.
I hold her and tell her how much I love her.
I pray with her, and I sing to her.
I do everything I can to keep her alert.

Thank you, Lord, for those flickering moments when
   Mom is rational and sane again.
I'm glad for every little glimpse of the person Mom
   used to be.
During those lucid times I know that this is the mother
   I'll meet in heaven someday.
Thank you, Father, for the happiness that this
   knowledge brings.

Amen.

for lucid moments

Does your loved one have difficulty focusing on the world around him or her? Tell God how that makes you feel, and ask him to help you enjoy the lucid moments. He can teach you to look past those things that hide your loved one's true personality. It may help to reflect on the relationship you've had in the past and look forward to the life you'll enjoy together someday in heaven.

The Swedish hymn "Thanks to God for My Redeemer" gives me
     something else, Lord, for which to be thankful—tears.
     Tears bring comfort, and tears bring healing.
     Thank you, God, for tears.

There are many tears that I've forgotten
          because they *did* comfort and heal.
     I know the tears came when I was a little girl
          and my puppy was killed.
     I know tears came when my "brother," Leslie,
          returned to Wisconsin after seven years
          of working on our farm.
     I know there were tears when we left family in Sweden
          to come home after a two-month visit.
     I know the tears came quickly when Grandma died.
Thank you, God, for giving me tears to help me through
          all of those times.

" *Thanks for tears*

Tears didn't come so easily after Dad died.
> At first I only felt relief that he was no longer suffering.
> I actually enjoyed the beautiful songs at Dad's funeral
>> because they reminded me of the love that Dad
>> had for music.
> It wasn't until the next day, as I listened alone to a tape
>> of the service, that I cried real tears.
Thank you, heavenly Father, for holding me in your arms
> when the tears finally came.

Once again it is difficult to let the tears flow as I grieve
> for Mom's lost ability to think and talk.
> Help me to be honest with you and always
>> let you know exactly how I feel.
> I know you'll hold me again as I cry to express
>> my sadness.
> Thank you, God, for tears.

In the name of Jesus, who wept for Jerusalem and
> for his friend Lazarus.

Amen.

by now forgotten "

Thank God for the tears you've been able to shed. At the same time, ask him to give you the freedom to stop holding back any tears that still need to flow. God will be there with you, to comfort and bring healing.

Prayers That Focus
on Jesus

*[Jesus said,] "Come to Me, all you who labor and
are heavy laden, and I will give you rest."*

MATTHEW 11:28, NKJV

Lord Jesus,

Yesterday I was a little girl, and you were my best Friend.
   When I learned to whistle, I practiced my new skill
      by whistling the tune of "Jesus Loves Me."
   When our family heard about a toddler who died,
      Mom told me he'd gone to heaven.
   I said I wanted to go there too.
   I didn't understand why Mom got upset
      and cried when I said that.

Today I'm an adult woman, and you are my best Friend.
   When I sing to myself, I sing songs that exalt and
      adore you, Jesus.
   After Dad died, I knew he had gone to be with you
      in heaven.
   I'm glad to know that I'll go to be with you someday too.
   I can't understand why some people look sad
      when I mention heaven.

Yesterday, today,

Tomorrow I'll be a retired senior citizen, and you'll
  still be my best Friend.
When I hum to myself, I'll hum tunes about your
  love and faithfulness, dear Jesus.
When I remember my life on this earth, I'll be thankful
  for all that you brought me through,
  and I'll look forward with great anticipation
    to all you have ahead for me.

Thank you, Jesus, for being my best Friend yesterday,
  today, and forever.
Thank you for dying for me in the past.
Thank you for living for me in the present.
Thank you for your promise that you'll be coming
  for me in the future.
You're the only Friend who will never leave me.

In your precious name I pray.

Amen.

and forever

As you go about your work today, tell Jesus how much you've enjoyed his friendship in the past, express your thanks for ways you enjoy his presence now, and let him know that you're looking forward to enjoying his promise for the future.

Turning my eyes toward Jesus

Jesus,

I want to focus on you.
Sometimes I am so weary when I come home
        from work, and Mom is so demanding.
        She doesn't understand the world around her.
        She forgets what I tell her before I finish talking.

I've read the story of Peter walking on water.
        He could do it as long as he kept his eyes on you.
        But when he turned his focus instead to the waves
            around him, he began to sink right down into
            the water.
        Fortunately, you were right there to save him!

Give me the desire and the ability to keep my focus
        on you.
Thank you for the example of my dad.
Even though he was legally blind, his favorite chorus
        was "Turn Your Eyes upon Jesus."
When "the things of earth" grew "strangely dim" for
        Dad, he enjoyed "the light" of your "glory
        and grace."

My vision needs adjusting today, Lord.
I've been focusing on the water around me,
        but I need to focus on you.
Thank you for being there.
Thank you for helping me to see you.

Amen.

What fearful "waters" do you find yourself focusing on? Close your eyes as you talk to Jesus—your living and loving Savior—about your fears. Focus on him, blocking out any fears or distractions.

Becoming like a child

Jesus,

You once said that everyone needs to become like a child.
    You said that's the only way to enter the kingdom
        of heaven.
Is that why you often allow older folks to regress until they
        are like children again?

After Mom had hip surgery her dementia worsened.
    When she was confused she would console herself
        by singing again and again, "Jesus Loves Me."
           Sometimes she sang all of the familiar words.
           Sometimes she made up her own.

Thank you, Jesus, for Mom's childlike faith.
Thank you for helping her recall songs about you
        that have brought comfort to her.

Mom often sits in the family room now,
        looking at the clouds and smiling.
    She sees you, Jesus, in those clouds, just as
        she saw you when she was a little girl.
    She knew you watched over her as a child,
        and she knows you're watching over her now.

Give me Mom's childlike faith, Lord.
    Help me to always trust you to watch over me.
    Comfort me with songs and Scriptures
        that remind me of your presence.

Amen.

Is your loved one becoming like a child? That can be upsetting, but try to thank the Lord Jesus for childlike faith. Ask for more of it for yourself and for your loved one. God's Word can bring you comfort as you deal with these changes.

Lord Jesus,

When you lived on this earth, your relationships with other
        people were very important to you.
    As a child you pleased your Father in heaven by
        obeying the mother and father he gave you on Earth.
    When you were dying on the cross, you looked down
        and saw your mother, Mary.
        At that moment you must have forgotten your
            own suffering.
        You saw how sad and alone your mother was,
            so you assigned John to be her caregiver.

During your ministry years, you encountered numerous
        people in need of care.
To each one, you reached out with love and compassion.
    You healed people who had been sick for many
        years.
    You brought vision to people who had never seen.
    You brought sound to people who had never heard.
    You brought life to people who had lost theirs.
    You gave new insights to the spiritually blind, deaf,
        and dumb.

Your example

Lord, I can't heal, bring vision, fix hearing, or give life.
But I can bring your love and compassion to Mom.
    I can be tender, kind, and understanding.
    I can entrust Mom to you.
    I can pray she will feel your love as well as mine.
    I can remind her of the good life you've given her
        and the incomprehensibly great life ahead.
    I can share Scriptures to help keep her spiritual
        eyes open.

Thank you, Jesus, for the example you have given me
        through your relationships with others.
I thank you that as I relate to my mother, I can put
        into practice what I'm learning from you.
Help me to become more like you each day,
        loving Mom and expressing that love
        as I care for her.

Amen.

is for me, Lord

Talk to Jesus about some ways the relationships he had on earth have given you an especially significant example to follow. Perhaps there is a specific area in which you wish you could be more like Jesus—such as relating to others with compassion, offering forgiveness, or trusting God completely. All you need to do is ask, and he will help you follow in his footsteps.

A very special place

Jesus,

You said you were going to prepare a place for your
children.
You said it would be a special place and it would be
where *you* are.
What could make it more special than that?
Thank you, Jesus, for this wonderful promise.

Many times when Dad used to wonder during the night
why you didn't take him home, I'd remind him
of your promise.
I'd say, "When Jesus is ready for you, he'll come."
Those words were always reassuring to Dad.

Thank you, Jesus, for wanting us to live with you.
Thank you for dying on the cross to make that
possible.
I'm thankful that even now you are preparing a place
for us, and that you will bring each of us there
at the perfect time.

In the name of Jesus the Son.

Amen.

*If your loved one has
accepted Christ, then
God is preparing a
place in heaven for him
or her. Ask God to help
you trust him to take
over the care of your
loved one when the
time is right.*

Prayers about Strength and Hope

I keep right on praying to you, Lord, hoping this is the time you will show me favor. . . . Pull me out of the mud; don't let me sink any deeper! . . . Don't let the floods overwhelm me, or the deep waters swallow me.

PSALM 69:13-15

Dear Lord Jesus,

Some people say there is a pot of gold at the end of each rainbow.
I doubt that, but I *do* know there are streets of gold at the
        end of life for each of your children.
    Dad's walking on one of them right now,
        probably taking care of the flowers alongside it.

Mom had a really bad morning today.
    She said I was the devil himself.
What should I do, Lord?
    One of Mom's medicines made her angry.
        Another made her very hyper.

At breakfast Mom spit out her food and wouldn't
        take her medicine.
I can't keep her with me if she forgets how to chew and swallow.
The days aren't getting better,
    and they will keep getting worse.
What should I do, Lord?
    I know that someday Mom will walk along those
        streets of gold with Dad.
    But I need some hope for today and for tomorrow.
        I need to know you're here right now.

Streets

Lord Jesus, it's later in the day, and now it's easy for me
        to see how good you are!
You knew I needed special encouragement today.
Just when I was at my wit's end at lunchtime, the home
        health-care doctor called.
He offered hope in the form of new medication
         that often helps to calm patients with dementia
      and has no side effects.

Thank you, Lord, for giving me the hope I needed today.
Such hope will keep me going until Mom is ready to walk
        on the streets of gold.
And it will keep me going until I reach those streets too.

Hallelujah! How I thank you, Jesus!

Amen.

of gold

Do you need some hope today? If your loved one is a believer, thank God for the streets of gold you'll walk on together someday. But also ask him for some hope that you can reach out and touch right now. Perhaps you should plan an evening out or a weekend getaway. God wants to give you the strength and hope you need as you travel with your loved one.

Dear Lord,

When Mom wakes up confused in the middle of the night,
    I don't know what to do.
    I put her on the commode, get her settled back in bed,
        and she just keeps talking, talking, talking.
I ask her to please be quiet—please let me sleep.

Father God, when I was young, I became upset with Mom
    for always telling me to get plenty of rest.
    Now if I tell *Mom* I need to get my rest
        because I have to get up early in the morning,
            she doesn't seem to care,
        and I can't reason with her.

Lord, even though I get upset with Mom for interrupting
    my sleep, in my heart I know it has nothing to do
    with her not caring.
    So I try to stroke Mom's face quietly, patiently, and
    lovingly as I encourage her to go back to sleep.

Night

You know I don't always succeed in being patient and loving
at three o'clock in the morning.
Please forgive me for the times I've let Mom know
she is a burden to me.
She may not understand what she is doing to upset me,
but her eyes show me she does understand when
I'm not happy with her.

Give me strength, Lord, to be kind and loving to Mom
when she wakes up during the night.
Give me the energy I need to focus on the work that
needs to be done the following day.
Please help Mom to relax and sleep the next night.

Thank you, Lord, for hearing and answering my prayer.

Amen.

thoughts

Are you able to get the rest you need? Ask God for strength when your loved one doesn't allow you to sleep through the night. You may also want to ask a doctor or nurse to recommend medications or bedtime routines that could help your loved one sleep.

Dear Lord,

I know some people grow old and enjoy having others
        wait on them.
But that's not how it was with my folks, Lord!
During more than twenty years of retirement both
        of them found joy and purpose in life.
    They found it in the things they were able to do
        for other people.

Then my parents gradually discovered they were no longer
        able to help so much,
    and they began to feel that their lives had no purpose.
I knew you didn't want them to feel that way, Father,
    so I tried to reiterate often how much it meant to me
        to have my parents with me.

Reason

I also told Mom and Dad how much I appreciated
  their prayers for me and for others.
Lord, I'm glad you gave me prayerful parents.
  While Mom was still able to work in the kitchen,
    she told me she would "send up" spontaneous
    little prayers all day long.
  Dad, who would lie on the sofa in the family room
    for hours at a time after he turned ninety, told me
    how he prayed for people, one by one.
  He prayed for family in America and in Sweden,
    for his church family, for neighbors, for friends
    nearby and out of state.

What greater purpose can there be than to pray for people,
  Lord?
Thank you that in their last years my parents continued
  to be helpful prayer warriors.

In the name of Jesus.

Amen.

to live

Does the person you care for seem to lack a purpose for living? Ask God to show you how to help your loved one feel needed. Remember that you have a purpose as well. For this season of your life, it may simply be to provide care and support for your loved one. Thank God that he can help each of you accept the purpose he has for you right now.

Dear God,

You've heard me offer excuses too often lately.
When I'm not as gentle with Mom as I ought to be,
I tell her I just can't handle it anymore.
When my words aren't as kind as they should be,
I tell Mom I'm too tired to be nice.

Then I talk to you, God, and I start to cry.
I recognize the missing fruit in my life—the fruit
of the Spirit.
Oh, Holy Spirit, please fill me with patience, kindness,
gentleness, and self-control.

I know you understand, and I know you forgive me.
But I don't want to hurt Mom by my words or
my actions.
I don't want to hurt you either, because I know you
do hurt—for Mom and for me—when I don't
allow your Spirit to have control.

Enjoying

Father God, I remember that a friend once told me why her
mother put her grandfather in a nursing home.
She did it because she didn't want to feel hatred
toward him.
I thought those were harsh words, Lord.
But when my body is exhausted and my emotions are
on a roller-coaster ride,
I understand what my friend's mother meant,
and that frightens me.

Lord, I need strength—physical, emotional, and spiritual.
I need to know when and how to make changes that will
help me relate to Mom in a way that pleases you.
Thank you for showing me when the fruit of your Spirit
is missing.
Please fill me so Mom will see your fruit in me.

In Jesus' name.

Amen.

God's fruit

Galatians 5:22-23 explains that "when the Holy Spirit controls our lives, he will produce this kind of fruit in us: love, joy, peace, patience, kindness, goodness, faithfulness, gentleness, and self-control." If you feel that some of these fruits of the Spirit are missing from your life, especially in this difficult time, ask God for help. He wants to provide the resources you need so that his fruit can grow and flourish in you.

Dear Lord,

How sad I was when my dad began losing his sight.
  I didn't know if he'd be able to cope.
I should have known that he would.

I remember, Lord, how Dad sold his *new* car to me
    and bought a *used* one for himself.
  He said it would be his last—it was.

The time finally came when Dad could no longer
    see well enough to drive at all.
Then he was confined to the house except for the days
    when someone took him for a ride.
He couldn't see his old fields across the road from
    where we had built our new house,
  but he told me, Lord, that he could picture himself
    driving through the country past all the
    familiar farms.

Contagious

He never lamented about what he couldn't see.
  He did praise you, God, for what he *could* see
    through the eyes of his memory.
  Thank you for the inner peace and contentment
    you provided for my dad.

During his final months, pain and medication
    sometimes made Dad feel downhearted.
But he was never completely hopeless, God.
He never stopped looking forward to better days with you.

How thankful I am that I was able to observe Dad
    as his time to leave us approached.
I watched a man who had walked and talked with you
    since his teenage years grow even closer to you.
I saw the physical man fade and the spiritual
    man blossom.
Thank you for the way my dad's hope in you has
    strengthened that hope in me.

In your precious Son's name.

Amen.

hope

Pray for God's peace and contentment to overflow in your loved one's life—and in yours. You might also ask God to help you select verses that will bring back hope if it has disappeared. (See Jeremiah 29:11 and Romans 8:38-39. You'll find these and other Scripture passages in the "Optional Worship Helps" section at the end of this book.)

Dear Father in heaven,

As Mom struggles through the dark valley
        of senility, I struggle with her.
I ache for her when she breathes heavily, her face
        gets red, and she becomes angry, lashing
        out at everyone around her.

She once asked me, "Where did I sleep last night?"
        "In your bedroom," I said.
        "I don't have a bedroom," she answered.

But in the midst of all this confusion, at a time when
        Mom could still speak, I would hear her talk
        to you, Lord.
And I'd hear the hope that was still within her.

Thank you for my mother's sweet faith expressed in
        the following prayer:
        "Father, take my body. Carry me to heaven.
        That's where I want to be.
        Hold me in your arms—press me to your heart.
        Oh, Father, I want to come to you.
        I will be so glad to see you face-to-face.

A lesson

Look down on me and say, 'Come, child, there is
    still room for you.'
You are the Holy Spirit, and I believe you.
    I can sit in your lap.
    I can have my heart delivered.
I believe in the love of Jesus,
    for he is the only one who can save our souls."

Then Mom spoke the words she heard Jesus say:
    "Welcome, little lady, at my side."
And Mom replied, "I know I am thine.
    I'm coming to you—maybe today!"

Thank you, Father, for allowing me to listen in on that
    conversation.
I know you'll help me recall it whenever I need the
    comfort of those words.

In the loving name of Jesus I pray.

Amen.

in hope

Do you need a lesson in hope? Then pray that God will help you learn it from the person you care for, from a friend, or from Scripture. And don't forget to thank God that he himself is "the God of hope" who can "fill you with all joy and peace as you trust in him" (Romans 15:13, NIV).

Dear Lord,

How well I remember the e-mail message I sent to many
    people shortly before Dad died.
  I titled it, "Time to Let Go."
Dad was keeping his eyes closed and refusing food.
  He spoke only three times that last week.

The first words Dad said that week were a response to my
    words, "Do you know what? I love you."
Usually he echoed, "Do you know what? I love you, too."
  This time he simply said, "I love thee."
Dad repeated those words a day later to Stephanie,
    the special little friend from church who had
      adopted my parents as grandparents.

Three days before Dad died, I recited the twenty-third Psalm
    and read Romans 8:15-38.
  Following every phrase of Scripture,
    there was a resounding Swedish "Ja! Ja!"

Time to

Dad knew you were waiting for him, Jesus, and he was
    excited about it.
I told him to be your little lamb and to follow you
    wherever you led him.
I said, "I love you, Dad, and I'm going to miss you,
    but it's okay."

He did follow you to your heavenly sheepfold, Lord.
    I stood by Dad's bed and said, "The pearly gates opened
        for you today, didn't they, Dad?"

Then I went home to Mom, who didn't understand
    what had happened.
But she listened and smiled as I read Psalm 16:11:
    "You will show me the way of life,
        granting me the joy of your presence
        and the pleasures of living with you forever."

Thank you, Lord, for the strength and the hope
    your words provide.

Amen.

let go

Do you need to ask for God's help so you'll be ready when the time comes for you to let go? If you begin talking to God about it now, you'll find it easier to receive comfort from God and his Word after your loved one enters the joy of God's presence. Some specific passages that might be helpful are John 14 and Revelation 21.

Optional Worship Helps for Caregiver and Care Receiver

N O T E   T O

THE READER

Do you ever wonder what to say or what to do when you try to spend a few moments of quality time with your elderly loved one? The following pages offer suggested prayers, Scripture readings, and songs that you may find suitable to share from time to time.

Here are some simple worship ideas that may be helpful.

PRAYERS FOR CARE RECEIVERS
- Six printed prayers will give you ideas of ways to help your care receiver talk to God.
- Pick out prayers, or portions of them, that seem appropriate for the current circumstances. Perhaps these prayers will act as a springboard allowing your loved one to express his or her own thoughts to God.

SCRIPTURE PASSAGES
- Choose Bible verses that have been favorites of your loved one. If you're not sure which ones they are, watch for responses as you read.
- Mark the Scripture passages in which your care receiver appears most interested, and don't hesitate to repeat the same ones over and over again.
- If your loved one has highlighted verses in his or her own Bible, select verses that the two of you can read together often.

SONGS
- Many elderly people have difficulty expressing their thoughts and feelings but can do so through music. So you'll want to check out the section of songs, which contains many timeless favorites.
- If you don't feel comfortable singing, you can still read the words. The rhythm of the poetry will very likely get the attention of the person you care for.

- You'll want to choose songs that your loved one knows. If you're not sure which ones those are, watch for a response as you sing or repeat the words.
- Mark the songs that your care receiver enjoys the most, and feel free to go back to the same ones again and again.
- If your loved one requests songs that aren't printed in this book, make a list of those songs along with the name of a songbook and the page number where you can find each one.
- Many churches record their services. If yours does, consider getting some of the tapes so you can play the music for your loved one. Or if you wish, ask if some of your church musicians would record favorite hymns, choruses, anthems, and other special music. Many recordings of hymns and praise songs are available from Christian bookstores, as well as on-line.

As you watch the moods of the person you care for, you'll recognize that there are days when a quiet worship time settles your loved one down. On those days you may spend half an hour singing, reading, and praying together.

On the other hand, there may be days when your parent or spouse struggles to understand reality or becomes emotionally distraught at any disruption of his or her routine. If that happens, don't force a worship time together.

Perhaps you care for a loved one who never committed his or her life to the Lord. Then ask for permission from time to time to read some of your favorite Scripture verses and to sing or repeat the words of some of your favorite songs. You can use the verses and songs as a way to share your personal testimony.

I pray that the following prayers, Scriptures, and songs will help you and your loved one experience meaningful worship times together.

Prayers for Care Receivers

O Lord, you alone are my hope.

Now, in my old age, don't set me aside.

I will keep on hoping for you to help me;

I will praise you more and more.

Psalm 71:5, 9, 14

Praise God, who gives all good gifts

Dear Father in heaven,

I thank you for the many years you have given to me.
You have been with me through good times and bad.
Thank you for never forgetting about me,
        even when I have forgotten about you.
I know you care about me.
    I know you are here with me right now.

I praise you for your love.
    It's such a perfect, pure, and holy love.
You showed me that love when you sent
        your Son, Jesus.
    Thank you, Jesus, for dying on the cross
        for my sins.
I want you to be my Shepherd.
    I want to be like a little lamb
        and follow you forever.

Amen.

Forgive me, Lord

Dear Lord,

You are so good.
    You know me, and still you love me.
You understand me too.
    You know what's in my heart.

Forgive me for the times I haven't trusted you.
Forgive me for the times I've been upset because
    I thought you should have handled things differently.

Lord God, help me to believe you know
    what's best.
Help me to believe you have everything
    under control.

Father, please forgive my sins.
    Cleanse me and purify me.
I want to be ready to meet you someday,
    whenever you're ready for me to come home.

Thank you for your one and only Son, Jesus,
    who came to be my Savior.
No one but Jesus is truly clean and pure.
I'm so glad he stands between you and me
    so that you see only his goodness
    when you look at me.

Amen.[1]

---

[1] Based on Einar Free's constant prayer the last six months of his life: Cleanse me, purify me, and make me whole.

Prayer of thanks for wonderful memories

Dear heavenly Father,

It's hard to feel thankful when I'm aching all over.
   And it's hard to express thankfulness when
      I'm lonely inside.
But I do have wonderful memories, Father God.
What blessings they are to me!
   I enjoy recalling many of those blessings
      every day.

There is my family, Lord.
We haven't been a perfect family—no family is.
   But we have had many good times together.
   Thank you for all of those special times.

Then there was my work.
   I always received great satisfaction
      from doing my best.
   Thank you for the work you allowed me to do.

I close my eyes and can still see the beauty of your world,
 my Creator-God.
  Thank you for the many different places
   I was able to visit.
I look again and see the wide variety of people in your
 world, all created in your image.
  Thank you, Father, for the many people who have
   been part of my life over the years.

Then there is the body of Christ.
I may not be able to attend church anymore—
  at least not without assistance.
  But I recall many happy Sunday mornings of worship,
   hours spent praying with other believers,
    and times others in my church family reached out
     to me in love.
  Thank you, Father, for the body of Christ.

My life has had its ups and downs,
  but you have never forgotten about me.
Help me never to forget about you or the wonderful
  memories with which you have blessed me.

In the wonderful name of Jesus I pray.

Amen.

Prayer for God's mercy

Dear Lord,

Sometimes I don't know what to do.
 I feel so tired and so helpless,
  and once in a while I get very confused.
 I stare into space, and the people around me act
  as if they think I'm crazy.
 Maybe I am.

Father, sometimes I feel as if I've been wandering
  in this desert long enough.
 I wait for you to carry me home,
  and yet you don't come, so I must wait
   and try not to grow too weary.
 Help me to rest quietly in the place you have
  provided until you come for me.
Thank you for keeping me safe and for offering
  your peace while I wait.

Lord, I know you are a merciful God.
I ask you to extend your mercy to me today.
 Give me strength when I feel weak.
 Give me courage when I feel depressed.
 Give me the grace to accept my limitations.

I love you, Lord, and I will praise you forever.
 I'll praise you for your mercy, for your love,
  for your understanding, and for your peace.

Amen.

Prayer of anticipation

Dear heavenly Father,

I'm looking forward to the time when I'll experience no
more pain or sadness or long nights.
Then there will be no reason for any more tears—
what a future!
How grateful I am, Lord, to know I can anticipate that
kind of future with you.
I can look up at the bright blue sky and imagine myself
going up to glory.
I can close my eyes and see myself walking down
golden streets with my Savior.

Sometimes it seems I've lived forever down here,
but I know life on earth is just the tip of the iceberg
compared to the life that will follow.
It will be good to be with you forever, dear Jesus.
What a wonderful, glorious, hallelujah day it will be
when you welcome me home.
I'm waiting, Jesus, as patiently as I can.[2]

Come quickly, Lord Jesus.

Amen.

[2]Based on Helen Free's many prayers anticipating her going home to Jesus.

Prayer for family and friends

Dear Lord,

I want to pray for my family.
> Each one means so much to me, even if I don't
> always remember names.

I pray for those in my immediate family and thank you
> for all they do for me.
> I know it's not always easy to take care of me.
> So I pray you will give them the strength they need
> for each day.

I pray for those in my extended family.
> You know each one by name, Father.
> You know which ones are your followers and
> which ones aren't.
> Bring them all into the fold before it's too late, Lord.

I pray for all of my friends, too, God.
> I thank you for the blessing that each one has been to me.
> Thank you for those who continue to befriend me even
> when I can't return the favor.
> Minister to each of them, Father, and bring them all
> home to you someday so we can be friends
> throughout eternity.

In the name of Jesus, the best Friend of all!

Amen.

The Lord's Prayer

You and your loved one may want to recite this familiar prayer together.

Our Father which art in heaven,
Hallowed be thy name.
Thy kingdom come.
Thy will be done in earth, as it is in heaven.
Give us this day our daily bread.
And forgive us our debts, as we forgive our debtors.
And lead us not into temptation, but deliver us from evil:
For thine is the kingdom, and the power, and the glory,
for ever.

Amen.

Matthew 6:9-13, KJV

Psalms

The Lord is my shepherd; I shall not want. He maketh me to lie
down in green pastures: he leadeth me beside the still waters.

PSALM 23:1-2, KJV

P S A L M   1   *Love for God's Word*

𝓑lessed is the man
 Who walks not in the counsel of the ungodly,
 Nor stands in the path of sinners,
 Nor sits in the seat of the scornful;
But his delight is in the law of the LORD,
 And in His law he meditates day and night.
He shall be like a tree
 Planted by the rivers of water,
 That brings forth its fruit in its season,
 Whose leaf also shall not wither;
And whatever he does shall prosper.

The ungodly are not so,
But are like the chaff which the wind drives away.
Therefore the ungodly shall not stand in the judgment,
Nor sinners in the congregation of the righteous.

For the LORD knows the way of the righteous,
But the way of the ungodly shall perish. (NKJV)

P S A L M   1 6 : 1 ,   5 - 1 1   *Hope and joy in God's presence*

𝓚eep me safe, O God,
 for I have come to you for refuge. . . .

LORD, you alone are my inheritance, my cup
 of blessing.
 You guard all that is mine
The land you have given me is a pleasant land.
 What a wonderful inheritance!

I will bless the LORD who guides me;
    even at night my heart instructs me.
I know the LORD is always with me.
    I will not be shaken, for he is right beside me.

No wonder my heart is filled with joy,
    and my mouth shouts his praises!
    My body rests in safety.
For you will not leave my soul among the dead
    or allow your godly one to rot in the grave.

You will show me the way of life,
    granting me the joy of your presence
    and the pleasures of living with you forever.

P S A L M   2 3   *Hope and peace from our Shepherd*

The LORD is my shepherd; I shall not want.
    He maketh me to lie down in green pastures: he leadeth me beside the still waters.
    He restoreth my soul: he leadeth me in the paths of righteousness for his name's sake.
    Yea, though I walk through the valley of the shadow of death, I will fear no evil: for thou art with me; thy rod and thy staff they comfort me.
    Thou preparest a table before me in the presence of mine enemies: thou anointest my head with oil; my cup runneth over.
    Surely goodness and mercy shall follow me all the days of my life: and I will dwell in the house of the LORD for ever. (KJV)

P S A L M   3 3 : 1 3 - 2 2   *Assurance of God's unfailing love*

*F*rom heaven the LORD looks down
 and sees all mankind;
from his dwelling place he watches
 all who live on earth—
he who forms the hearts of all,
 who considers everything they do.
No king is saved by the size of his army;
 no warrior escapes by his great strength.
A horse is a vain hope for deliverance;
 despite all its great strength it cannot save.
But the eyes of the LORD are on those who fear him,
 on those whose hope is in his unfailing love,
to deliver them from death
 and keep them alive in famine.
We wait in hope for the LORD;
 he is our help and our shield.
In him our hearts rejoice,
 for we trust in his holy name.
May your unfailing love rest upon us, O LORD,
 even as we put our hope in you. (NIV)

P S A L M   3 4 : 3 - 8 ,   1 8 - 1 9   *Trusting God even in suffering*

*C*ome, let us tell of the LORD's greatness;
 let us exalt his name together.
I prayed to the LORD, and he answered me,
 freeing me from all my fears.
Those who look to him for help will be radiant with joy;
 no shadow of shame will darken their faces.
I cried out to the LORD in my suffering, and he heard me.

He set me free from all my fears.
For the angel of the LORD guards all who fear him,
    and he rescues them.
Taste and see that the LORD is good.
    Oh, the joys of those who trust in him! . . .
The LORD is close to the brokenhearted;
    he rescues those who are crushed in spirit.
The righteous face many troubles,
    but the LORD rescues them from each and every one.

PSALM 37:3-6 *Committing everything to God*

Trust in the LORD and do good.
    Then you will live safely in the land and prosper.
Take delight in the LORD,
    and he will give you your heart's desires.

Commit everything you do to the LORD.
    Trust him, and he will help you.
He will make your innocence as clear as the dawn,
    and the justice of your cause will shine
    like the noonday sun.

PSALM 40:1-3, 11-13 *Waiting patiently for God's rescue*

I waited patiently for the LORD to help me,
    and he turned to me and heard my cry.
He lifted me out of the pit of despair,
    out of the mud and the mire.
He set my feet on solid ground
    and steadied me as I walked along.

He has given me a new song to sing,
    a hymn of praise to our God.
Many will see what he has done and be astounded.
    They will put their trust in the LORD. . . .
LORD, don't hold back your tender mercies from me.
    My only hope is in your unfailing love and faithfulness.
For troubles surround me—
    too many to count!
They pile up so high
    I can't see my way out.
They are more numerous than the hairs on my head.
    I have lost all my courage.
Please, LORD, rescue me!

PSALM 42:1-2, 5-6 *Longing for God*

As the deer pants for streams of water,
    so my soul pants for you, O God.
My soul thirsts for God, for the living God. . . .
Why are you downcast, O my soul?
    Why so disturbed within me?
Put your hope in God,
    for I will yet praise him,
        my Savior and my God. (NIV)

PSALM 46:1-2 *God's help and strength*

God is our refuge and strength, a very present help in trouble. Therefore will not we fear, though the earth be removed, and though the mountains be carried into the midst of the sea. (KJV)

PSALM 51:1-2, 10-12   *God's compassion and forgiveness*

Have mercy upon me, O God,
　According to Your lovingkindness;
According to the multitude of Your tender mercies,
Blot out my transgressions.
Wash me thoroughly from my iniquity,
And cleanse me from my sin. . . .

Create in me a clean heart, O God,
And renew a steadfast spirit within me.
Do not cast me away from Your presence,
And do not take Your Holy Spirit from me.

Restore to me the joy of Your salvation,
And uphold me by Your generous Spirit. (NKJV)

PSALM 61:1-5   *God is a safe refuge*

Hear my cry, O God;
　listen to my prayer.

From the ends of the earth I call to you,
　　I call as my heart grows faint;
　　lead me to the rock that is higher than I.
For you have been my refuge,
　　a strong tower against the foe.

I long to dwell in your tent forever
　　and take refuge in the shelter of your wings.
For you have heard my vows, O God;
　　you have given me the heritage of those who fear your
　　name. (NIV)

PSALM 71:5-11, 14-23   *Hope and strength in old age*

O Lord, you alone are my hope.
    I've trusted you, O LORD, from childhood.
Yes, you have been with me from birth;
    from my mother's womb you have cared for me.
No wonder I am always praising you!

My life is an example to many,
    because you have been my strength and protection.
That is why I can never stop praising you;
    I declare your glory all day long.

And now, in my old age, don't set me aside.
    Don't abandon me when my strength is failing.
For my enemies are whispering against me.
    They are plotting together to kill me.
They say, "God has abandoned him.
    Let's go and get him,
    for there is no one to help him now." . . .

But I will keep on hoping for you to help me;
    I will praise you more and more.
I will tell everyone about your righteousness.
    All day long I will proclaim your saving power,
    for I am overwhelmed by how much
    you have done for me.
I will praise your mighty deeds, O Sovereign LORD.
    I will tell everyone that you alone are just and good.

O God, you have taught me from my earliest childhood,
    and I have constantly told others about the
    wonderful things you do.

Now that I am old and gray,
    do not abandon me, O God.
Let me proclaim your power to this new generation,
    your mighty miracles to all who come after me.

Your righteousness, O God, reaches to the
    highest heavens.
      You have done such wonderful things.
      Who can compare with you, O God?
You have allowed me to suffer much hardship,
    but you will restore me to life again
    and lift me up from the depths of the earth.
You will restore me to even greater honor
    and comfort me once again.

Then I will praise you with music on the harp,
    because you are faithful to your promises, O God.
I will sing for you with a lyre,
    O Holy One of Israel.
I will shout for joy and sing your praises,
    for you have redeemed me.

PSALM 84:1-4, 10-12   *Longing for God*

How lovely is your dwelling place,
    O LORD Almighty!
My soul yearns, even faints,
    for the courts of the LORD;
my heart and my flesh cry out
    for the living God.
Even the sparrow has found a home,
    and the swallow a nest for herself,

where she may have her young—
a place near your altar,
O LORD Almighty, my King and my God.
Blessed are those who dwell in your house;
they are ever praising you. . . .
Better is one day in your courts
than a thousand elsewhere;
I would rather be a doorkeeper in the house of my God
than dwell in the tents of the wicked.
For the LORD God is a sun and shield;
the LORD bestows favor and honor;
no good thing does he withhold
from those whose walk is blameless.
O LORD Almighty,
blessed is the man who trusts in you. (NIV)

PSALM 90:1-4, 10, 12, 14   *Numbering our days*

Lord, you have been our dwelling place
throughout all generations.
Before the mountains were born
or you brought forth the earth and the world,
from everlasting to everlasting you are God.

You turn men back to dust,
saying, "Return to dust, O sons of men."
For a thousand years in your sight
are like a day that has just gone by,
or like a watch in the night. . . .

The length of our days is seventy years—
or eighty, if we have the strength;

yet their span is but trouble
    and sorrow,
        for they quickly pass, and we fly away. . . .

Teach us to number our days aright,
    that we may gain a heart of wisdom. . . .

Satisfy us in the morning with your unfailing love,
    that we may sing for joy and be glad all our days. (NIV)

PSALM 95:1-7   *Praise for God's greatness*

Come, let us sing to the LORD!
    Let us give a joyous shout to the rock of our
    salvation!
Let us come before him with thanksgiving.
    Let us sing him psalms of praise.
For the LORD is a great God,
    the great King above all gods.
He owns the depths of the earth,
    and even the mightiest mountains are his.
The sea belongs to him, for he made it.
    His hands formed the dry land, too.
Come, let us worship and bow down.
    Let us kneel before the LORD our maker,
    for he is our God.
We are the people he watches over,
    the sheep under his care.

Oh, that you would listen to his voice
    today!

PSALM 100   *Praise for God's goodness*

$\mathcal{M}$ake a joyful noise unto the LORD, all ye lands.

Serve the LORD with gladness: come before his presence with singing.

Know ye that the LORD he is God: it is he that hath made us, and not we ourselves; we are his people, and the sheep of his pasture.

Enter into his gates with thanksgiving, and into his courts with praise: be thankful unto him, and bless his name.

For the LORD is good; his mercy is everlasting; and his truth endureth to all generations. (KJV)

PSALM 103:1-6, 10-18
Praise for God's love and understanding

$\mathcal{B}$less the LORD, O my soul;
And all that is within me, bless His holy name!
Bless the LORD, O my soul,
And forget not all His benefits:
Who forgives all your iniquities,
Who heals all your diseases,
Who redeems your life from destruction,
Who crowns you with lovingkindness and tender mercies,
Who satisfies your mouth with good things,
So that your youth is renewed like the eagle's.

The LORD executes righteousness
And justice for all who are oppressed. . . .
He has not dealt with us according to our sins,
Nor punished us according to our iniquities.

For as the heavens are high above the earth,
So great is His mercy toward those who fear Him;
As far as the east is from the west,
So far has He removed our transgressions from us.
As a father pities his children,
So the LORD pities those who fear Him.
For He knows our frame;
He remembers that we are dust.

As for man, his days are like grass;
As a flower of the field, so he flourishes.
For the wind passes over it, and it is gone,
And its place remembers it no more.
But the mercy of the LORD is from everlasting to everlasting
On those who fear Him,
And His righteousness to children's children,
To such as keep His covenant,
And to those who remember His commandments to do
    them. (NKJV)

PSALM 119:11, 103, 105-112
Loving and obeying God's Word

I have hidden your word in my heart
    that I might not sin against you. . . .
How sweet are your words to my taste,
    sweeter than honey to my mouth! . . .
Your word is a lamp to my feet
    and a light for my path.
I have taken an oath and confirmed it,
    that I will follow your righteous laws.
I have suffered much;

preserve my life, O LORD, according to your word.
Accept, O LORD, the willing praise of my mouth,
    and teach me your laws.
Though I constantly take my life in my hands,
    I will not forget your law.
The wicked have set a snare for me,
    but I have not strayed from your precepts.
Your statutes are my heritage forever;
    they are the joy of my heart.
My heart is set on keeping your decrees
    to the very end. (NIV)

PSALM 121 *God's care and help*

I look up to the mountains—
    does my help come from there?
My help comes from the LORD,
    who made the heavens and the earth!
He will not let you stumble and fall;
    the one who watches over you will not sleep.
Indeed, he who watches over Israel
    never tires and never sleeps.
The LORD himself watches over you!
    The LORD stands beside you as your protective
        shade.
The sun will not hurt you by day,
    nor the moon at night.
The LORD keeps you from all evil
    and preserves your life.
The LORD keeps watch over you as you come and go,
    both now and forever.

PSALM 139:1-12, 16-18, 23-24

God knows us and never leaves us

O LORD, you have searched me
  and you know me.
You know when I sit and when I rise;
  you perceive my thoughts from afar.
You discern my going out and my lying down;
  you are familiar with all my ways.
Before a wORD is on my tongue
  you know it completely, O LORD.

You hem me in—behind and before;
  you have laid your hand upon me.
Such knowledge is too wonderful for me,
  too lofty for me to attain.

Where can I go from your Spirit?
  Where can I flee from your presence?
If I go up to the heavens, you are there;
  if I make my bed in the depths, you are there.
If I rise on the wings of the dawn,
  if I settle on the far side of the sea,
even there your hand will guide me,
  your right hand will hold me fast.

If I say, "Surely the darkness will hide me
  and the light become night around me,"
even the darkness will not be dark to you;
  the night will shine like the day,
  for darkness is as light to you. . . .

All the days ordained for me
    were written in your book
    before one of them came to be.

How precious to me are your thoughts, O God!
    How vast is the sum of them!
Were I to count them,
    they would outnumber the grains of sand.
When I awake,
    I am still with you. . . .

Search me, O God, and know my heart;
    test me and know my anxious thoughts.
See if there is any offensive way in me,
    and lead me in the way everlasting. (NIV)

P s a l m   1 4 4 : 3 - 4 ,   7   *Deliverance from our troubles*

*L*ORD, what is man, that You take knowledge of him?
Or the son of man, that You are mindful of him?
Man is like a breath;
his days are like a passing shadow. . . .

Stretch out Your hand from above;
Rescue me and deliver me out of great waters. (NKJV)

P s a l m   1 4 5   *Sharing God's greatness with the next generation*

I will praise you, my God and King,
    and bless your name forever and ever.
I will bless you every day,

and I will praise you forever.
Great is the LORD! He is most worthy of praise!
    His greatness is beyond discovery!
Let each generation tell its children
    of your mighty acts.
I will meditate on your majestic, glorious splendor
    and your wonderful miracles.
Your awe-inspiring deeds will be on every tongue;
    I will proclaim your greatness.
Everyone will share the story of your wonderful goodness;
    they will sing with joy of your righteousness.
The LORD is kind and merciful,
    slow to get angry, full of unfailing love.
The LORD is good to everyone.
    He showers compassion on all his creation.
All of your works will thank you, LORD,
    and your faithful followers will bless you.
They will talk together about the glory of your kingdom;
    they will celebrate examples of your power.
They will tell about your mighty deeds
    and about the majesty and glory of your reign.
For your kingdom is an everlasting kingdom.
    You rule generation after generation.

The LORD is faithful in all he says;
    he is gracious in all he does.
The LORD helps the fallen
    and lifts up those bent beneath their loads.
All eyes look to you for help;
    you give them their food as they need it.
When you open your hand,
    you satisfy the hunger and thirst of every living thing.
The LORD is righteous in everything he does;

he is filled with kindness.
The LORD is close to all who call on him,
    yes, to all who call on him sincerely.
He fulfills the desires of those who fear him;
    he hears their cries for help and rescues them.
The LORD protects all those who love him,
    but he destroys the wicked.
I will praise the LORD,
    and everyone on earth will bless his holy name
    forever and forever.

PSALM 148 *All creation praises God*

Praise the LORD!

Praise the LORD from the heavens!
    Praise him from the skies!
Praise him, all his angels!
    Praise him, all the armies of heaven!
Praise him, sun and moon!
    Praise him, all you twinkling stars!
Praise him, skies above!
    Praise him, vapors high above the clouds!
Let every created thing give praise to the LORD,
    for he issued his command, and they came into being.
He established them forever and forever.
    His orders will never be revoked.
Praise the LORD from the earth,
    you creatures of the ocean depths,
fire and hail, snow and storm,
    wind and weather that obey him,
mountains and all hills,

fruit trees and all cedars,
wild animals and all livestock,
    reptiles and birds,
kings of the earth and all people,
    rulers and judges of the earth,
young men and maidens,
    old men and children.
Let them all praise the name of the LORD.
    For his name is very great;
    his glory towers over the earth and heaven!
He has made his people strong,
    honoring his godly ones—
    the people of Israel who are close to him.

Praise the LORD!

PSALM 150 *Everything that breathes praises God*

*P*raise the LORD.

Praise God in his sanctuary;
    praise him in his mighty heavens.
Praise him for his acts of power;
    praise him for his surpassing greatness.
Praise him with the sounding of the trumpet,
    praise him with the harp and lyre,
praise him with tambourine and dancing,
    praise him with the strings and flute,
praise him with the clash of cymbals,
    praise him with resounding cymbals.
Let everything that has breath praise the LORD.

Praise the LORD. (NIV)

Other Favorite Scriptures

For God so loved the world, that he gave his only begotten Son, that whosoever believeth in him should not perish, but have everlasting life.

John 3:16, KJV

P R O V E R B S   3 : 5 - 6   *Trusting God to lead us*

*T*rust in the LORD with all thine heart; and lean not unto thine own understanding. In all thy ways acknowledge him, and he shall direct thy paths. (KJV)

I S A I A H   4 0 : 2 8 - 3 1   *Relying on God for strength*

*H*ave you not known?
Have you not heard?
The everlasting God, the LORD,
The Creator of the ends of the earth,
Neither faints nor is weary.
His understanding is unsearchable.
He gives power to the weak,
And to those who have no might He increases strength.
Even the youths shall faint and be weary,
And the young men shall utterly fall,
But those who wait on the LORD
Shall renew their strength;
They shall mount up with wings like eagles,
They shall run and not be weary,
They shall walk and not faint. (NKJV)

I S A I A H   5 5 : 1 ,   6 - 7   *Longing for God, seeking forgiveness*

*E*veryone who thirsts, come to the waters. . . .

Seek the LORD while He may be found;
Call upon Him while He is near.
Let the wicked forsake his way,

And the unrighteous man his thoughts;
Let him return to the LORD,
And He will have mercy on him;
And to our God,
For He will abundantly pardon. (NKJV)

JEREMIAH 29:11-13 *Believing God's plans are good*

For I know the plans I have for you," declares the LORD, "plans to prosper you and not to harm you, plans to give you hope and a future. Then you will call upon me and come and pray to me, and I will listen to you. You will seek me and find me when you seek me with all your heart." (NIV)

LAMENTATIONS 3:19-26, 31-32
Grieving over loss, trusting in God's faithfulness

The thought of my suffering and homelessness is bitter beyond words. I will never forget this awful time, as I grieve over my loss. Yet I still dare to hope when I remember this:

The unfailing love of the LORD never ends! By his mercies we have been kept from complete destruction. Great is his faithfulness; his mercies begin afresh each day. I say to myself, "The LORD is my inheritance; therefore, I will hope in him!"

The LORD is wonderfully good to those who wait for him and seek him. So it is good to wait quietly for salvation from the LORD. . . .

For the LORD does not abandon anyone forever. Though he brings grief, he also shows compassion according to the greatness of his unfailing love.

MALACHI 4:1-2   *Freedom and joy for God's children*

*T*he LORD Almighty says, "The day of judgment is coming, burning like a furnace. The arrogant and the wicked will be burned up like straw on that day. They will be consumed like a tree—roots and all.

"But for you who fear my name, the Sun of Righteousness will rise with healing in his wings. And you will go free, leaping with joy like calves let out to pasture."

MATTHEW 6:25-30   *God's provision*

*S*o I tell you, don't worry about everyday life—whether you have enough food, drink, and clothes. Doesn't life consist of more than food and clothing? Look at the birds. They don't need to plant or harvest or put food in barns because your heavenly Father feeds them. And you are far more valuable to him than they are. Can all your worries add a single moment to your life? Of course not.

And why worry about your clothes? Look at the lilies and how they grow. They don't work or make their clothing, yet Solomon in all his glory was not dressed as beautifully as they are. And if God cares so wonderfully for flowers that are here today and gone tomorrow, won't he more surely care for you?

MATTHEW 11:28-30   *Spiritual rest through Jesus*

*C*ome to Me, all you who labor and are heavy laden, and I will give you rest. Take My yoke upon you and learn from Me, for I am gentle and lowly in heart, and you will find rest for your souls. For My yoke is easy and My burden is light. (NKJV)

MATTHEW 28:5-6, 18-20
Jesus lives and will always be with us

Then the angel spoke to the women. "Don't be afraid!" he said. "I know you are looking for Jesus, who was crucified. He isn't here! He has been raised from the dead, just as he said would happen. . . ."

Jesus came and told his disciples, "I have been given complete authority in heaven and on earth. Therefore, go and make disciples of all the nations, baptizing them in the name of the Father and the Son and the Holy Spirit. Teach these new disciples to obey all the commands I have given you. And be sure of this: I am with you always, even to the end of the age."

JOHN 3:16-17 *Salvation through God's Son*

For God so loved the world, that he gave his only begotten Son, that whosoever believeth in him should not perish, but have everlasting life. For God sent not his Son into the world to condemn the world; but that the world through him might be saved. (KJV)

JOHN 10:7-16 *Safety with the Good Shepherd*

I assure you, I am the gate for the sheep," [Jesus] said. "All others who came before me were thieves and robbers. But the true sheep did not listen to them. Yes, I am the gate. Those who come in through me will be saved. Wherever they go, they will find green pastures. The thief's purpose is to steal and kill and destroy. My purpose is to give life in all its fullness.

"I am the good shepherd. The good shepherd lays down his life for the sheep. A hired hand will run when he sees a wolf coming. He will leave the sheep because they aren't his and he isn't their shepherd. And so the wolf attacks them and scatters the flock. The hired hand runs away because he is merely hired and has no real concern for the sheep.

"I am the good shepherd; I know my own sheep, and they know me, just as my Father knows me and I know the Father. And I lay down my life for the sheep. I have other sheep, too, that are not in this sheepfold. I must bring them also, and they will listen to my voice; and there will be one flock with one shepherd."

JOHN 14:1-3, 6, 18-19   *Jesus prepares a place*

*L*et not your heart be troubled; you believe in God, believe also in Me. In My Father's house are many mansions; if it were not so, I would have told you. I go to prepare a place for you. And if I go and prepare a place for you, I will come again and receive you to Myself; that where I am, there you may be also. . . .

I am the way, the truth, and the life. No one comes to the Father except through me. . . .

I will not leave you orphans; I will come to you.

A little while longer and the world will see Me no more, but you will see Me. Because I live, you will live also. (NKJV)

ROMANS 5:1-11   *Learning from trials, becoming God's friends*

*T*herefore, since we have been made right in God's sight by faith, we have peace with God because of what Jesus Christ our LORD has done for us. Because of our faith, Christ has brought us into this place of highest privilege where we now stand, and we confidently and joyfully look forward to sharing God's glory.

We can rejoice, too, when we run into problems and trials, for we know that they are good for us—they help us learn to endure. And endurance develops strength of character in us, and character strengthens our confident expectation of salvation. And this expectation will not disappoint us. For we know how dearly God loves us, because he has given us the Holy Spirit to fill our hearts with his love.

When we were utterly helpless, Christ came at just the right time and died for us sinners. . . . God showed his great love for us by sending Christ to die for us while we were still sinners. And since we have been made right in God's sight by the blood of Christ, he will certainly save us from God's judgment. For since we were restored to friendship with God by the death of his Son while we were still his enemies, we will certainly be delivered from eternal punishment by his life. So now we can rejoice in our wonderful new relationship with God—all because of what our LORD Jesus Christ has done for us in making us friends of God.

ROMANS 8:16-24 *Release from suffering*

We are God's children. And since we are his children, we will share his treasures—for everything God gives to his Son, Christ, is ours, too. But if we are to share his glory, we must also share his suffering.

Yet what we suffer now is nothing compared to the glory he will give us later. . . . All creation anticipates the day when it will join God's children in glorious freedom from death and decay. . . . Even we Christians, although we have the

Holy Spirit within us as a foretaste of future glory, also groan to be released from pain and suffering. We, too, wait anxiously for that day when God will give us our full rights as his children, including the new bodies he has promised us. Now that we are saved, we eagerly look forward to this freedom.

ROMANS 8:35, 37-39   *No separation from Christ's love*

*W*ho shall separate us from the love of Christ? Shall trouble or hardship or persecution or famine or nakedness or danger or sword? . . . No, in all these things we are more than conquerors through him who loved us. For I am convinced that neither death nor life, neither angels nor demons, neither the present nor the future, nor any powers, neither height nor depth, nor anything else in all creation, will be able to separate us from the love of God that is in Christ Jesus our Lord. (NIV)

EPHESIANS 2:8-9   *God's gift of salvation*

*F*or it is by grace you have been saved, through faith—and this not from yourselves, it is the gift of God—not by works, so that no one can boast. (NIV)

PHILIPPIANS 3:8-14
Knowing Christ, reaching the end of the race

*Y*es, everything else is worthless when compared with the priceless gain of knowing Christ Jesus my Lord. I have discarded everything else, counting it all as garbage, so that

I may have Christ and become one with him. I no longer count on my own goodness or my ability to obey God's law, but I trust Christ to save me. For God's way of making us right with himself depends on faith. As a result, I can really know Christ and experience the mighty power that raised him from the dead. I can learn what it means to suffer with him, sharing in his death, so that, somehow, I can experience the resurrection from the dead!

I don't mean to say that I have already achieved these things or that I have already reached perfection! But I keep working toward that day when I will finally be all that Christ Jesus saved me for and wants me to be. No, dear brothers and sisters, I am still not all I should be, but I am focusing all my energies on this one thing: Forgetting the past and looking forward to what lies ahead, I strain to reach the end of the race and receive the prize for which God, through Christ Jesus, is calling us up to heaven.

PHILIPPIANS 4:4-9

Praying with thanksgiving, God's peace

*R*ejoice in the LORD always. I will say it again: Rejoice! Let your gentleness be evident to all. The LORD is near. Do not be anxious about anything, but in everything, by prayer and petition, with thanksgiving, present your requests to God. And the peace of God, which transcends all understanding, will guard your hearts and your minds in Christ Jesus.

Finally, brothers, whatever is true, whatever is noble, whatever is right, whatever is pure, whatever is lovely, whatever is admirable—if anything is excellent or praiseworthy—think about such things. Whatever you have learned or received or heard from me, or seen in me—put it into practice. And the God of peace will be with you. (NIV)

1 Thessalonians 4:13-18
Meeting Jesus in the clouds

I do not want you to be ignorant, brethren, concerning those who have fallen asleep, lest you sorrow as others who have no hope. For if we believe that Jesus died and rose again, even so God will bring with Him those who sleep in Jesus.

For this we say to you by the word of the Lord, that we who are alive and remain until the coming of the Lord will by no means precede those who are asleep. For the Lord Himself will descend from heaven with a shout, with the voice of an archangel, and with the trumpet of God. And the dead in Christ will rise first. Then we who are alive and remain shall be caught up together with them in the clouds to meet the Lord in the air. And thus we shall always be with the Lord. Therefore comfort one another with these words. (NKJV)

Hebrews 13:8 *Jesus never changes*

J esus Christ is the same yesterday and today and forever. (NIV)

James 1:12 *Crown of life*

B lessed is the man who perseveres under trial, because when he has stood the test, he will receive the crown of life that God has promised to those who love him. (NIV)

REVELATION 3:20 *Jesus knocks at our heart's door*

$\mathcal{B}$ehold, I stand at the door and knock. If anyone hears My voice and opens the door, I will come in to him and dine with him, and he with Me. (NKJV)

REVELATION 21:1-6, 10-11, 22-27
Looking forward to heaven

$\mathcal{T}$hen I saw a new heaven and a new earth, for the old heaven and the old earth had disappeared. And the sea was also gone. And I saw the holy city, the new Jerusalem, coming down from God out of heaven like a beautiful bride prepared for her husband.

I heard a loud shout from the throne, saying, "Look, the home of God is now among his people! He will live with them, and they will be his people. God himself will be with them. He will remove all of their sorrows, and there will be no more death or sorrow or crying or pain. For the old world and its evils are gone forever."

And the one sitting on the throne said, "Look, I am making all things new!" And then he said to me, "Write this down, for what I tell you is trustworthy and true." And he also said, "It is finished! I am the Alpha and the Omega— the Beginning and the End. To all who are thirsty I will give the springs of the water of life without charge! . . ."

So he took me in spirit to a great, high mountain, and he showed me the holy city, Jerusalem, descending out of heaven from God. It was filled with the glory of God and sparkled like a precious gem, crystal clear like jasper. . . .

No temple could be seen in the city, for the Lord God Almighty and the Lamb are its temple. And the city has no need of sun or moon, for the glory of God illuminates the city, and the Lamb is its light. The nations of the earth will walk in its light, and the rulers of the world will come and bring their glory to it. Its gates never close at the end of day because there is no night. And all the nations will bring their glory and honor into the city. Nothing evil will be allowed to enter—no one who practices shameful idolatry and dishonesty—but only those whose names are written in the Lamb's Book of Life.

Hymns and
Spiritual Songs

Speak to one another with psalms, hymns and spiritual songs.

Sing and make music in your heart to the Lord.

EPHESIANS 5:19, NIV

A Wonderful Savior Is Jesus My Lord

Fanny Jane Crosby (1820–1915)

A wonderful Savior is Jesus my Lord,
A wonderful Savior to me;
He hideth my soul in the cleft of the rock,
Where rivers of pleasure I see.

He hideth my soul in the cleft of the rock
That shadows a dry, thirsty land;
He hideth my life in the depths of His love,
And covers me there with His hand,
And covers me there with His hand.

A wonderful Savior is Jesus my Lord,
He taketh my burden away;
He holdeth me up, and I shall not be moved,
He giveth me strength as my day.

With numberless blessings each moment He crowns,
And, filled with His fulness divine,
I sing in my rapture, "O glory to God
For such a Redeemer as mine!"

When clothed in His brightness transported I rise,
To meet Him in clouds of the sky,
His perfect salvation, His wonderful love,
I'll shout with the millions on high.

All the Way My Savior Leads Me

Fanny Jane Crosby (1820–1915)

All the way my Savior leads me;
What have I to ask beside?
Can I doubt His tender mercy,
Who through life has been my guide?
Heav'nly peace, divinest comfort,
Here by faith in Him to dwell!
For I know whate'er befall me,
Jesus doeth all things well;
For I know whate'er befall me,
Jesus doeth all things well.

All the way my Savior leads me;
Cheers each winding path I tread,
Gives me grace for ev'ry trial,
Feeds me with the living bread:
Though my weary steps may falter,
And my soul athirst may be,
Gushing from the Rock before me,
Lo! a spring of joy I see;
Gushing from the Rock before me,
Lo! a spring of joy I see.

All the way my Savior leads me;
Oh, the fullness of His love!
Perfect rest to me is promised
In my Father's house above:
When my spirit, cloth'd immortal,
Wings its flight to realms of day,
This my song through endless ages:
Jesus led me all the way;
This my song through endless ages:
Jesus led me all the way.

Amazing Grace

John Newton (1725–1807); stanza 5: John P. Rees (1828–1900)

Amazing grace! how sweet the sound—
That saved a wretch like me!
I once was lost but now am found,
Was blind but now I see.

'Twas grace that taught my heart to fear,
And grace my fears relieved;
How precious did that grace appear
The hour I first believed!

The LORD has promised good to me,
His WORD my hope secures;
He will my shield and portion be
As long as life endures.

Through many dangers, toils and snares
I have already come;
'Tis grace hath brought me safe thus far,
And grace will lead me home.

When we've been there ten thousand years,
Bright shining as the sun,
We've no less days to sing God's praise
Than when we'd first begun.

Be Still, My Soul

Katharina Amalia von Schlegel (1697–?)
Translated by Jane Laurie Borthwick (1813–1897)

Be still, my soul! the LORD is on thy side;
Bear patiently the cross of grief or pain;
Leave to thy God to order and provide;
In every change He faithful will remain.
Be still, my soul! thy best, thy heavenly Friend
Through thorny ways leads to a joyful end.

Be still, my soul! thy God doth undertake
To guide the future as He has the past.
Thy hope, thy confidence let nothing shake;
All now mysterious shall be bright at last.
Be still, my soul! the waves and winds still know
His voice who ruled them while He dwelt below.

Be still, my soul! the hour is hastening on
When we shall be forever with the Lord,
When disappointment, grief, and fear are gone,
Sorrow forgot, love's purest joys restored.
Be still, my soul! when change and tears are past,
All safe and blessed we shall meet at last.

Blessed Assurance

Fanny Jane Crosby (1820–1915)

Blessed assurance, Jesus is mine!
O what a foretaste of glory divine!
Heir of salvation, purchase of God,
Born of His Spirit, washed in His blood.

This is my story, this is my song,
Praising my Savior all the day long;
This is my story, this is my song,
Praising my Savior all the day long.

Perfect submission, perfect delight!
Visions of rapture now burst on my sight;
Angels descending bring from above
Echoes of mercy, whispers of love.

Perfect submission—all is at rest,
I in my Savior am happy and blest;
Watching and waiting, looking above,
Filled with His goodness, lost in His love.

Children of the Heavenly Father

Carolina Sandell Berg (1832–1903)
Translated by Ernst W. Olson (1870–1958)

Children of the heav'nly Father
Safely in His bosom gather;
Nestling bird nor star in heaven
Such a refuge e'er was given.

God His own doth tend and nourish,
In His holy courts they flourish;
From all evil things He spares them,
In His mighty arms He bears them.

Neither life nor death shall ever
From the LORD His children sever;
Unto them His grace He showeth,
And their sorrows all He knoweth.

Praise the LORD in joyful numbers,
Your protector never slumbers;
At the will of your Defender
Ev'ry foe-man must surrender.

Though He giveth or He taketh,
God His children ne'er forsaketh;
His the loving purpose solely
To preserve them pure and holy.

Cleanse Me

James Edwin Orr (1912–1987)

Search me, O God, and know my heart today;
Try me, O Savior, know my thoughts, I pray.
See if there be some wicked way in me;
Cleanse me from every sin, and set me free.

I praise Thee, Lord, for cleansing me from sin;
Fulfill Thy Word, and make me pure within.
Fill me with fire, where once I burned with shame;
Grant my desire to magnify Thy name.

Lord, take my life, and make it wholly Thine;
Fill my poor heart with Thy great love divine.
Take all my will, my passion, self and pride;
I now surrender, Lord—in me abide.

O Holy Ghost, revival comes from Thee;
Send a revival, start the work in me.
Thy WORD declares Thou wilt supply our need;
For blessings now, O Lord, I humbly plead.

Day by Day and with Each Passing Moment

Carolina Sandell Berg (1832–1903)
Translated by Andrew L. Skoog (1856–1934)

Day by day and with each passing moment,
Strength I find to meet my trials here;
Trusting in my Father's wise bestowment,
I've no cause for worry or for fear.
He whose heart is kind beyond all measure
Gives unto each day what He deems best—
Lovingly, its part of pain and pleasure,
Mingling toil with peace and rest.

Ev'ry day the LORD Himself is near me
With a special mercy for each hour;
All my cares He fain would bear, and cheer me,
He whose name is Counsellor and Pow'r.
The protection of His child and treasure
Is a charge that on Himself He laid;
"As thy day, thy strength shall be in measure,"
This the pledge to me He made.

Help me then in ev'ry tribulation
So to trust Thy promises, O Lord,
That I lose not faith's sweet consolation
Offered me within Thy holy Word.
Help me, Lord, when toil and trouble meeting,
E'er to take, as from a father's hand,
One by one, the days, the moments fleeting,
Till I reach the promised land.

Great Is Thy Faithfulness

Thomas Obadiah Chisholm (1866–1960)

Great is Thy faithfulness, O God my Father,
There is no shadow of turning with Thee;
Thou changest not, Thy compassions they fail not;
As Thou hast been Thou forever wilt be.

Great is Thy faithfulness!
Great is Thy faithfulness!
Morning by morning new mercies I see;
All I have needed Thy hand hath provided—
Great is Thy faithfulness, Lord, unto me!

Summer and winter, and springtime and harvest,
Sun, moon and stars in their courses above
Join with all nature in manifold witness
To Thy great faithfulness, mercy and love.

Pardon for sin and a peace that endureth,
Thy own dear presence to cheer and to guide;
Strength for today and bright hope for tomorrow,
Blessings all mine, with ten thousand beside!

Have Thine Own Way, Lord!

Adelaide Addison Pollard (1862–1934)

Have Thine own way, Lord! Have Thine own way!
Thou art the potter; I am the clay.
Mold me and make me after Thy will,
While I am waiting, yielded and still.

Have Thine own way, Lord! Have Thine own way!
Search me and try me, Master, today!
Whiter than snow, Lord, wash me just now,
As in Thy presence humbly I bow.

Have Thine own way, Lord! Have Thine own way!
Wounded and weary, help me, I pray!
Power, all power, surely is Thine!
Touch me and heal me, Savior divine!

Have Thine own way, Lord! Have Thine own way!
Hold o'er my being absolute sway!
Fill with Thy Spirit till all shall see
Christ only, always, living in me!

How Great Thou Art

Stuart K. Hine (1899–1989)

O LORD my God! When I in awesome wonder
Consider all the *worlds Thy hands have made.
I see the stars, I hear the *rolling thunder,
Thy power throughout the universe displayed.

Then sings my soul, my Savior God to Thee:
HOW GREAT THOU ART! HOW GREAT THOU ART!
Then sings my soul, my Savior God to Thee:
HOW GREAT THOU ART! HOW GREAT THOU ART.

When through the woods and forest glades I wander
And hear the birds sing sweetly in the trees,
When I look down from lofty mountain grandeur
And hear the brook and feel the gentle breeze.

And when I think that God, His Son not sparing,
Sent Him to die, I scarce can take it in;
That on the cross, my burden gladly bearing,
He bled and died to take away my sin.

When Christ shall come with shout of acclamation
And take me home, what joy shall fill my heart!
Then I shall bow in humble adoration
And there proclaim, my God HOW GREAT THOU ART!

*Author's original words are "works" and "mighty."

I Need Thee Every Hour

Annie Sherwood Hawks (1835–1918); refrain, Robert Lowry (1826–1899)

I need Thee ev'ry hour,
Most gracious Lord;
No tender voice like Thine
Can peace afford.

I need Thee, O I need Thee;
Ev'ry hour I need Thee!
O bless me now, my Savior,
I come to Thee.

I need Thee ev'ry hour,
Stay Thou nearby;
Temptations lose their pow'r
When Thou art nigh.

I need Thee ev'ry hour,
In joy or pain;
Come quickly, and abide,
Or life is vain.

I need Thee ev'ry hour,
Teach me Thy will,
And Thy rich promises
In me fulfill.

I Surrender All

Judson W. Van De Venter (1855–1939)

All to Jesus I surrender,
All to Him I freely give;
I will ever love and trust Him,
In His presence daily live.

I surrender all,
I surrender all.
All to Thee, my blessed Savior,
I surrender all.

All to Jesus I surrender,
Humbly at His feet I bow,
Worldly pleasures all forsaken,
Take me, Jesus, take me now.

All to Jesus I surrender,
Make me, Savior, wholly Thine;
May Thy Holy Spirit fill me,
May I know Thy pow'r divine.

All to Jesus I surrender,
Lord, I give myself to Thee;
Fill me with Thy love and power,
Let Thy blessing fall on me.

It Is Well with My Soul

Horatio Gates SpaffORD (1828–1888)

When peace like a river attendeth my way,
When sorrows like sea-billows roll;
Whatever my lot, Thou hast taught me to say,
"It is well, it is well with my soul."

It is well with my soul,
It is well, it is well with my soul.

Though Satan should buffet, tho' trials should come,
Let this blest assurance control,
That Christ has regarded my helpless estate,
And hath shed His own blood for my soul.

My sin—O, the bliss of this glorious thought,
My sin—not in part but the whole,
Is nailed to the cross and I bear it no more,
Praise the Lord, praise the Lord, O my soul!

And, Lord, haste the day when the faith shall be sight,
The clouds be rolled back as a scroll,
The trump shall resound and the LORD shall descend,
"Even so"—it is well with my soul.

Jesus Calls Us

Cecil Frances Alexander (1818–1895)

Jesus calls us; o'er the tumult
Of our life's wild, restless sea,
Day by day His sweet voice soundeth,
Saying, "Christian, follow Me."

Jesus calls us from the worship
Of the vain world's golden store,
From each idol that would keep us,
Saying, "Christian, love Me more."

In our joys and in our sorrows,
Days of toil and hours of ease,
Still He calls in cares and pleasures,
"Christian, love Me more than these."

Jesus calls us: by Thy mercies,
Savior, may we hear Thy call,
Give our hearts to Thine obedience,
Serve and love Thee best of all.

Jesus Loves Me

Anna Bartlett Warner (1820–1915)

Jesus loves me! this I know,
For the Bible tells me so;
Little ones to Him belong,
They are weak but He is strong.

Yes, Jesus loves me!
Yes, Jesus loves me!
Yes, Jesus loves me!
The Bible tells me so.

Jesus loves me! He who died
Heaven's gate to open wide;
He will wash away my sin,
Let His little child come in.

Jesus loves me! He will stay
Close beside me all the way;
Thou hast bled and died for me,
I will henceforth live for Thee.

Just a Closer Walk with Thee

Author unknown

I am weak but Thou art strong;
Jesus, keep me from all wrong;
I'll be satisfied as long
As I walk, let me walk close to Thee.

Just a closer walk with Thee,
Grant it, Jesus, is my plea,
Daily, walking close to Thee,
Let it be, dear Lord, let it be.

Through this world of toil and snares,
If I falter, Lord, who cares?
Who with me my burden shares?
None but Thee, dear Lord, none but Thee.

When my feeble life is o'er,
Time for me will be no more;
Guide me gently, safely o'er
To Thy kingdom shore, to Thy shore.

Just As I Am

Charlotte Elliott (1789–1871)
Stanzas 1-3, 5

Just as I am, without one plea,
But that Thy blood was shed for me,
And that Thou bidd'st me come to Thee,
O Lamb of God I come! I come!

Just as I am, and waiting not
To rid my soul of one dark blot,
To Thee, whose blood can cleanse each spot,
O Lamb of God I come! I come!

Just as I am, tho' tossed about
With many a conflict, many a doubt,
Fightings within, and fears without,
O Lamb of God I come! I come!

Just as I am, Thou wilt receive,
Wilt welcome, pardon, cleanse, relieve;
Because Thy promise I believe,
O Lamb of God I come! I come!

Leaning on the Everlasting Arms

Elisha Albright Hoffman (1839–1929)

What a fellowship, what a joy divine,
Leaning on the everlasting arms;
What a blessedness, what a peace is mine,
Leaning on the everlasting arms.

Leaning, leaning,
Safe and secure from all alarms;
Leaning, leaning,
Leaning on the everlasting arms.

O, how sweet to walk in this pilgrim way,
Leaning on the everlasting arms;
O, how bright the path grows from day to day,
Leaning on the everlasting arms.

What have I to dread, what have I to fear,
Leaning on the everlasting arms?
I have blessed peace with my LORD so near,
Leaning on the everlasting arms.

Like a River Glorious

Frances Ridley Havergal (1836–1879)

Like a river glorious
Is God's perfect peace,
Over all victorious
In its bright increase;
Perfect, yet it floweth
Fuller ev'ry day,
Perfect, yet it groweth
Deeper all the way.

Stayed upon Jehovah,
Hearts are fully blest—
Finding as He promised
Perfect peace and rest.

Hidden in the hollow
Of His blessed hand,
Never foe can follow,
Never traitor stand;
Not a surge of worry,
Not a shade of care,
Not a blast of hurry
Touch the spirit there.

Ev'ry joy or trial
Falleth from above,
Traced upon our dial
By the sun of love;
We may trust Him fully
All for us to do—
They who trust Him wholly
Find Him wholly true.

My Faith Has Found a Resting Place

Lidie H. Edmunds (1851–1920)

My faith has found a resting place—
Not in device or creed:
I trust the Ever-Living One—
His wounds for me shall plead.

I need no other argument,
I need no other plea;
It is enough that Jesus died,
And that He died for me.

Enough for me that Jesus saves—
This ends my fear and doubt;
A sinful soul I come to Him—
He'll never cast me out.

My heart is leaning on the Word—
The written WORD of God:
Salvation by my Savior's name—
Salvation through His blood.

My great Physician heals the sick—
The lost He came to save;
For me His precious blood He shed—
For me His life He gave.

My Jesus, I Love Thee

William Ralph Featherston (1846–1873)

My Jesus, I love Thee, I know Thou art mine—
For Thee all the follies of sin I resign;
My gracious Redeemer, my Savior art Thou:
If ever I loved Thee, my Jesus, 'tis now.

I love Thee because Thou hast first loved me
And purchased my pardon on Calvary's tree;
I love Thee for wearing the thorns on Thy brow:
If ever I loved Thee, my Jesus, 'tis now.

I'll love Thee in life, I will love Thee in death,
And praise Thee as long as Thou lendest me breath;
And say when the death-dew lies cold on my brow,
"If ever I loved Thee, my Jesus, 'tis now."

In mansions of glory and endless delight,
I'll ever adore Thee in heaven so bright;
I'll sing with the glittering crown on my brow,
"If ever I loved Thee, my Jesus, 'tis now."

Near to the Heart of God

Cleland Boyd McAfee (1866–1944)

There is a place of quiet rest
Near to the heart of God,
A place where sin cannot molest,
Near to the heart of God.

O Jesus, blest Redeemer,
Sent from the heart of God,
Hold us who wait before Thee
Near to the heart of God.

There is a place of comfort sweet
Near to the heart of God,
A place where we our Savior meet,
Near to the heart of God.

There is a place of full release
Near to the heart of God,
A place where all is joy and peace,
Near to the heart of God.

O God, Our Help in Ages Past

Isaac Watts (1674–1748)

O God, our help in ages past,
Our hope for years to come,
Our shelter from the stormy blast,
And our eternal home!

Under the shadow of Thy throne
Still may we dwell secure;
Sufficient is Thine arm alone,
And our defense is sure.

Before the hills in order stood,
Or earth received her frame,
From everlasting Thou art God,
To endless years the same.

A thousand ages in Thy sight
Are like an evening gone;
Short as the watch that ends the night,
Before the rising sun.

Time, like an ever-rolling stream,
Bears all its sons away;
They fly, forgotten, as a dream
Dies at the opening day.

O God, our help in ages past,
Our hope for years to come;
Be Thou our guide while life shall last,
And our eternal home.

O Jesus, I Have Promised

John Ernest Bode (1816–1874)

O Jesus, I have promised
To serve Thee to the end;
Be Thou forever near me,
My Master and my Friend:
I shall not fear the battle
If Thou art by my side,
Nor wander from the pathway
If Thou wilt be my guide.

O let me feel Thee near me,
The world is ever near;
I see the sights that dazzle,
The tempting sounds I hear:
My foes are ever near me,
Around me and within;
But, Jesus, draw Thou nearer,
And shield my soul from sin.

O Jesus, Thou has promised
To all who follow Thee,
That where Thou art in glory,
There shall Thy servant be;
And, Jesus, I have promised
To serve Thee to the end;
O give me grace to follow,
My Master and my Friend.

Out of My Bondage, Sorrow, and Night

William T. Sleeper (1819–1904)
Stanzas 1-2, 4

Out of my bondage, sorrow, and night,
Jesus, I come, Jesus, I come;
Into thy freedom, gladness, and light,
Jesus, I come to thee.
Out of my sickness into thy health,
Out of my want and into thy wealth,
Out of my sin and into thyself,
Jesus, I come to thee.

Out of my shameful failure and loss,
Jesus, I come, Jesus, I come;
Into the glorious gain of thy cross,
Jesus, I come to thee.
Out of earth's sorrows into thy balm,
Out of life's storms and into thy calm,
Out of distress to jubilant psalm,
Jesus, I come to thee.

Out of the fear and dread of the tomb,
Jesus, I come, Jesus, I come;
Into the joy and light of thy home,
Jesus, I come to thee.
Out of the depths of ruin untold,
Into the peace of thy sheltering fold,
Ever thy glorious face to behold,
Jesus, I come to thee.

Rock of Ages

Augustus Toplady (1740–1778)

Rock of Ages, cleft for me,
Let me hide myself in Thee;
Let the water and the blood,
From Thy wounded side which flowed,
Be of sin the double cure,
Save from wrath and make me pure.

Could my tears forever flow,
Could my zeal no languor know,
These for sin could not atone;
Thou must save, and Thou alone.
In my hand no price I bring;
Simply to Thy cross I cling.

While I draw this fleeting breath,
When my eyes shall close in death,
When I rise to worlds unknown,
And behold Thee on Thy throne,
Rock of Ages, cleft for me,
Let me hide myself in Thee.

Savior, Like a Shepherd Lead Us

Hymns for the Young, 1836
Attributed to Dorothy A. Thrupp (1779–1847)

Savior, like a shepherd lead us,
Much we need Thy tender care;
In Thy pleasant pastures feed us,
For our use Thy folds prepare:
Blessed Jesus, blessed Jesus!
Thou hast bought us, Thine we are.

We are Thine, do Thou befriend us,
Be the guardian of our way;
Keep Thy flock, from sin defend us,
Seek us when we go astray:
Blessed Jesus, blessed Jesus!
Hear, O hear us, when we pray.

Thou hast promised to receive us,
Poor and sinful though we be;
Thou hast mercy to relieve us,
Grace to cleanse and power to free:
Blessed Jesus, blessed Jesus!
Early let us turn to Thee.

Early let us seek Thy favor,
Early let us do Thy will;
Blessed LORD and only Savior,
With Thy love our bosoms fill:
Blessed Jesus, blessed Jesus!
Thou hast loved us, love us still.

Softly and Tenderly Jesus Is Calling

William Lamartine Thompson (1847–1909)

Softly and tenderly Jesus is calling,
Calling for you and for me;
See, on the portals He's waiting and watching,
Watching for you and for me.

Come home, come home,
Ye who are weary, come home;
Earnestly, tenderly, Jesus is calling,
Calling, O sinner, come home!

Why should we tarry when Jesus is pleading,
Pleading for you and for me?
Why should we linger and heed not His mercies,
Mercies for you and for me?

Time is now fleeting, the moments are passing,
Passing from you and from me;
Shadows are gathering, death's night is coming,
Coming for you and for me.

O for the wonderful love He has promised,
Promised for you and for me!
Though we have sinned, He has mercy and pardon,
Pardon for you and for me.

Take Time to Be Holy

William Dunn Longstaff (1822–1894)

Take time to be holy,
Speak oft with thy Lord;
Abide in Him always,
And feed on His Word.
Make friends of God's children;
Help those who are weak;
Forgetting in nothing
His blessing to seek.

Take time to be holy,
The world rushes on;
Much time spend in secret
With Jesus alone;
By looking to Jesus,
Like Him thou shalt be;
Thy friends in thy conduct
His likeness shall see.

Take time to be holy,
Let Him be thy guide,
And run not before Him
Whatever betide;
In joy or in sorrow
Still follow the Lord,
And, looking to Jesus,
Still trust in His Word.

Take time to be holy,
Be calm in thy soul;
Each thought and each motive
Beneath His control;
Thus led by His Spirit
To fountains of love,
Thou soon shalt be fitted
For service above.

Thanks to God for My Redeemer

August Ludwig Storm (1862–1914)
Translated by Carl E. Backstrom (1901–)

Thanks to God for my Redeemer,
Thanks for all Thou dost provide!
Thanks for times now but a memory,
Thanks for Jesus by my side!
Thanks for pleasant, balmy springtime,
Thanks for dark and dreary fall!
Thanks for tears by now forgotten,
Thanks for peace within my soul!

Thanks for prayers that Thou has answered,
Thanks for what Thou dost deny!
Thanks for storms that I have weathered,
Thanks for all Thou dost supply!
Thanks for pain and thanks for pleasure,
Thanks for comfort in despair!
Thanks for grace that none can measure,
Thanks for love beyond compare!

Thanks for roses by the wayside,
Thanks for thorns their stems contain!
Thanks for home and thanks for fireside,
Thanks for hope, that sweet refrain!
Thanks for joy and thanks for sorrow,
Thanks for heav'nly peace with Thee!
Thanks for hope in the tomorrow,
Thanks through all eternity!

The Old Rugged Cross

George Bennard (1873–1958)

On a hill far away stood an old
  rugged cross,
The emblem of suffering and shame;
And I love that old cross where the
  dearest and best
For a world of lost sinners was slain.

So I'll cherish the old rugged cross,
'Til my trophies at last I lay down;
I will cling to the old rugged cross,
And exchange it some day for a crown.

O that old rugged cross, so despised
  by the world,
Has a wondrous attraction for me;
For the dear Lamb of God left His
  glory above
To bear it to dark Calvary.

In the old rugged cross, stained with
  blood so divine,
A wondrous beauty I see;
For 'twas on that old cross Jesus
  suffered and died
To pardon and sanctify me.

To the old rugged cross I will ever be
  true,
Its shame and reproach gladly bear;
Then He'll call me some day to my
  home far away,
Where His glory forever I'll share.

Trust and Obey

John H. Sammis (1846–1919)

When we walk with the LORD in the light of His Word,
What a glory He sheds on our way!
While we do His good will He abides with us still,
And with all who will trust and obey.

Trust and obey, for there's no other way
To be happy in Jesus, but to trust and obey.

Not a shadow can rise, not a cloud in the skies,
But His smile quickly drives it away;
Not a doubt nor a fear, not a sigh nor a tear,
Can abide while we trust and obey.

Not a burden we bear, not a sorrow we share,
But our toil He doth richly repay;
Not a grief nor a loss, not a frown nor a cross,
But is blest if we trust and obey.

But we never can prove the delights of His love
Until all on the altar we lay;
For the favor He shows and the joy He bestows
Are for them who will trust and obey.

Then in fellowship sweet we will sit at His feet,
Or we'll walk by His side in the way;
What He says we will do, where He sends we will go—
Never fear, only trust and obey.

Under His Wings I Am Safely Abiding

William Orcutt Cushing (1823–1902)

Under His wings I am safely abiding;
Though the night deepens and tempests are wild,
Still I can trust Him—I know He will keep me;
He has redeemed me and I am His child.

Under His wings, under His wings,
Who from His love can sever?
Under His wings my soul shall abide,
Safely abide forever.

Under His wings, what a refuge in sorrow!
How the heart yearningly turns to His rest!
Often when earth has no balm for my healing,
There I find comfort and there I am blest.

Under His wings, O what precious enjoyment!
There will I hide till life's trials are o'er;
Sheltered, protected, no evil can harm me;
Resting in Jesus I'm safe evermore.

What a Friend We Have in Jesus

Joseph Medlicott Scriven (1819–1886)

What a Friend we have in Jesus,
All our sins and griefs to bear!
What a privilege to carry
Everything to God in prayer!
O what peace we often forfeit,
O what needless pain we bear,
All because we do not carry
Everything to God in prayer!

Have we trials and temptations?
Is there trouble anywhere?
We should never be discouraged,
Take it to the LORD in prayer.
Can we find a friend so faithful
Who will all our sorrows share?
Jesus knows our every weakness,
Take it to the LORD in prayer.

Are we weak and heavy-laden,
Cumbered with a load of care?
Precious Savior, still our refuge—
Take it to the LORD in prayer.
Do thy friends despise, forsake thee?
Take it to the LORD in prayer;
In His arms He'll take and shield thee,
Thou wilt find a solace there.

Psalm 1 120

Psalm 16:1, 5-11 120

Psalm 23 121

Psalm 33:13-22 122

Psalm 34:3-8, 18-19 122

Psalm 37:3-6 123

Psalm 40:1-3, 11-13 123

Psalm 42:1-2, 5-6 124

Psalm 46:1-2 124

Psalm 51:1-2, 10-12 125

Psalm 61:1-5 125

Psalm 71:5-11, 14-23 126

Psalm 84:1-4, 10-12 127

Psalm 90:1-4, 10, 12, 14 128

Psalm 95:1-7 129

Psalm 100 130

Psalm 103:1-6, 10-18 130

Psalm 119:11, 103, 105-112 131

Psalm 121 132

Psalm 139:1-12, 16-18, 23-24 133

Psalm 144:3-4, 7 134

Psalm 145 134

Psalm 148 136

Psalm 150 137

Proverbs 3:5-6 140

Isaiah 40:28-31 140

Isaiah 55:1, 6-7 140

Jeremiah 29:11-13 141

Lamentations 3:19-26, 31-32 141

Malachi 4:1-2 142

Matthew 6:25-30 142

Matthew 11:28-30 142

Matthew 28:5-6, 18-20 143

John 3:16-17 143

John 10:7-16 143

John 14:1-3, 6, 18-19 144

Romans 5:1-11 144

Romans 8:16-24 145

Romans 8:35, 37-39 146

Ephesians 2:8-9 146

Philippians 3:8-14 146

Philippians 4:4-9 147

1 Thessalonians 4:13-18 148

Hebrews 13:8 148

James 1:12 148

Revelation 3:20 149

Revelation 21:1-6, 10-11, 22-27 149

A Wonderful Savior Is Jesus My Lord . . 152

All the Way My Savior Leads Me 153

Amazing Grace 154

Be Still, My Soul 155

Blessed Assurance 156

Children of the Heavenly Father 157

Cleanse Me 158

Day by Day and with Each Passing
    Moment 159

Great Is Thy Faithfulness 160

Have Thine Own Way, Lord! 161

How Great Thou Art 162

I Need Thee Every Hour 163

I Surrender All 164

It Is Well with My Soul 165

Jesus Calls Us 166

Jesus Loves Me 167

Just a Closer Walk with Thee 168

Just As I Am 169

Leaning on the Everlasting Arms 170

Like a River Glorious 171

My Faith Has Found a Resting Place . . 172

My Jesus, I Love Thee 173

Near to the Heart of God 174

O God, Our Help in Ages Past 175

O Jesus, I Have Promised 176

Out of My Bondage, Sorrow, and Night . 177

Rock of Ages 178

Savior, Like a Shepherd Lead Us 179

Softly and Tenderly Jesus Is Calling . . . 180

Take Time to Be Holy 181

Thanks to God for My Redeemer 182

The Old Rugged Cross 183

Trust and Obey 184

Under His Wings I Am Safely Abiding . 185

What a Friend We Have in Jesus 186

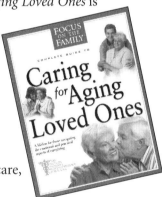